The Write Genre

Classroom activities and mini-lessons that promote writing with clarity, style and flashes of brilliance

LORI JAMISON ROG

PAUL KROPP

Pembroke Publishers Limited

Paul would like to dedicate this book to C. Reid Sanders, who taught him much of what he knows about writing in Rm. 227 of Hutch-Tech some 40 years ago.

Lori would like to dedicate this book to her mother, Hertha Jamison, who was good at writing . . . and everything else.

© 2004 Pembroke Publishers
538 Hood Road
Markham, Ontario, Canada L3R 3K9
www.pembrokepublishers.com

Distributed in the U.S. by Stenhouse Publishers
480 Congress Street
Portland, ME 04101
www.stenhouse.com

We acknowledge the financial support of the Government of Canada through the Book Publishing Industry Development Program (BPIDP) for our publishing activities.

We acknowledge the Government of Ontario through the Ontario Media Development Corporation's Ontario Book Initiative.

National Library of Canada Cataloguing in Publication

Rog, Lori, 1955-
   The write genre : classroom activities and mini-lessons that promote writing with clarity, style and flashes of brilliance / Lori Jamison Rog, Paul Kropp.

Includes bibliographical references and index.
ISBN 1-55138-172-9

   1. English language — Composition and exercises — Study and teaching (Elementary) I. Kropp, Paul, 1948- II. Title.

LB1528.R63 2004   372.62'3044   C2004-902674-7

Editor: Kate Revington
Cover Design: John Zehethofer
Cover Photography: Ajay Photographics
Typesetting: Jay Tee Graphics Ltd.

Printed and bound in Canada
9 8 7 6

Acknowledgments

The authors would like to thank many teachers and colleagues who commented on various portions of the text. These include Wilfred Burton, Tim Caleval, Lynn Fluter, Shelly Galloway, Laurie Gatzke, Andrea Hnatiuk, Dawn Kesslering, Trudy Loftsgard, Greg Smith and Dianne Stark. As well, we would like to thank our friends in the "IRA Club" for their ongoing advice and encouragement, particularly Connie Watson, Donna Koch, Wilfred Burton, Gloria Antifaiff, Gregg Kurek, Becky Olness, Donna Ogle and Jeanne Paratore.

We would also like to thank the South Saskatchewan Reading Council for permission to reprint student writing samples from their *Young Saskatchewan Writers* publications.

Contents

Introduction

Think about the kinds of writing you do in your life: reports, notes, memos, instructions, lists, business proposals, agendas, reference letters, resumés, calendars . . . the list is long. As adults, all of us are writers, but we're primarily writers of nonfiction. Even in our house, where Paul makes his living writing novels for young adults, he spends much of his day on many other kinds of writing. What does a working novelist do when he's not working on a book? He writes reports, notes, memos, instructions, lists, business proposals, agendas, letters, resumés and calendars.

Our point is simple. If our goal as teachers is to provide students with lifelong literacy skills, we must ensure that they are exposed to a variety of forms and genres of text. Although most of the reading and writing we do in elementary school is narrative, most of the reading and writing we do as adults is expository. Both types of writing are important for our students to become successful writers throughout their lives.

Writing with Purpose and Audience in Mind

All of us write best when we have a purpose for writing and we know someone is going to read what we've written. When we want to remember four or five things to pick up at the grocery store after school, we write a list, not a descriptive paragraph. When we write a letter of complaint to the manufacturer of a defective product, we describe the problem and outline our requirements for compensation; we don't send a poem. When we send a postcard to a friend, we write a short vacation memoir, not a professional resumé.

If student writing is to be purposeful and "authentic," our students must learn the structures, formats, language and style that are most appropriate for the writing tasks they will ultimately face. Our job is to teach them how.

When Donald Graves, Nancie Atwell, Lucy Calkins and other teacher-researchers began to tell us about a writer's process more than a decade go, many of us interpreted their advice as a hands-off approach to writing instruction. We saw our role as teachers to create the environment, provide the opportunity to write, and offer response to what was written. Decisions about topic and genre, revision and editing, and publishing or not lay solely in the hands of the student.

As a result, many of our students were writing a lot *more*, but not necessarily writing a lot *better*.

While we still advocate student ownership and choice, we now know that a "balanced" writing program must include instruction in the elements of both craft and conventions. This instruction may take the form of brief mini-lessons or longer maxi-lessons, may be done with the whole class or by individual coaching, and should be presented in a variety of styles and formats. But, whatever form your lesson takes, it should be directly connected to a meaningful writing experience. For students to become better writers, they need an immediate opportunity to practise what is taught and enough time to craft purposeful writing that someone is actually going to read.

A balanced writing program has three key elements:
- assigned writing
- self-selected writing
- writing to learn

As with all aspects of your language arts program, *balance* is the key to effective teaching and learning. Balanced writing instruction includes full-scale assignments carried through all stages of the writing process, as well as short exercises to practise a skill and to encourage fluency and experimentation. But teacher-directed assignments are only one component of the balanced writing program. Students must also have opportunities to engage in self-selected writing and writing to learn.

Whatever the writing form or genre, it must be explicitly taught, carefully modeled and extensively practised in a safe and supportive writing environment. This, and this alone, will make your students better writers.

A Framework for Teaching Many Genres of Text

The Write Genre is designed to help teachers organize their writing programs around the text forms that our children will be using for the rest of their lives. We use the word "genre" to identify the following six kinds of text:

- personal memoir
- fictional narrative
- informational report
- opinion writing
- procedural writing
- poetry

In this book, we offer tools and techniques, ideas and mini-lessons for teaching each of these genres within the framework of the writing process.

The first two chapters contain ideas for implementing a process approach to writing and ways to organize your classroom routines for success. Chapter 3 describes the Six Traits rubric, a powerful tool that links assessment and instruction. Chapters 4 to 9 are organized around systematic teaching and practice in each of the six featured genres. The final chapter describes a unique culminating activity – the multi-genre project – that will give your students a chance to work with all the text forms you've taught them through the year.

In every chapter, we offer ideas for pre-writing, drafting, revising and publishing. More than 50 mini-lessons are provided to help teachers present aspects of process, style and craft. Each chapter concludes with a set of reproducible resource pages that may be used as posters or as teaching aids for classroom use.

Student writing samples are also included in each genre chapter. These are models – both good and not-so-good – of what students have written. The samples may be reproduced to give your own students practice in revising someone else's work.

In *The Write Genre*, we have integrated a Writing Workshop approach with systematic instruction in a wide variety of writing tasks. In each chapter, we provide the scaffolds that students need in order to understand how writing differs for different purposes and audiences. Throughout, our book is designed to give you lessons to hone the craft of writing in many genres.

Not all of your students will grow up to write eloquent articles for national magazines or professional journals, but they can all learn to write with clarity, style and flashes of brilliance. It all begins with good teaching.

1

How Writers Really Write – The Writing Process

Before you read any further, take a minute to do this quick exercise. Imagine for a moment that you have to stop at the grocery store and pick up four or five items. Write yourself a reminder of what you need to buy. For example:

Bread   Grapes
Chkn   Dressing
Ice crm

Now imagine that something has come up so you can't do the shopping yourself. Someone else has to do your shopping for you. Make whatever changes you need in order to ensure that the person understands what you want. Your list might look like this:

Multigrain bread, sliced, the store brand
Boneless chicken breasts (if they're on sale, otherwise don't bother)
Rollo ice cream (the big container)
Green grapes (about 2 lbs)
Creamy Cucumber Salad Dressing (Kraft)

Let's look at the process of this communication. Before you began, you probably made a decision – a kind of pre-writing – to write the reminder in the *form* of a list. Lists serve a particular purpose: they provide the key information without extraneous detail.

Next, you *drafted* your list. You might not have written it very neatly – after all, a list, by definition, is quick to write – and it probably had scanty detail and even a few abbreviations or misspellings. That was fine as long as you were the only one who was going to read it. But when you realized that someone else was going to read and act upon your notes, you had to make some changes. You realized that your reader would need more information on some items. As soon as you

As long as you're the only audience for your writing, a one-draft wonder is just fine. If someone else is going to read it, you'd better follow the writing process.

began adding detail – changing your text to suit an outside audience – you were involved in *revising*.

Revising a shopping list doesn't call for much. You have to explain what kind of items you usually buy (multigrain bread, not white) and give some provisos on expense (only buy the chicken breasts if they're on sale). Finally, you might fix up any careless spelling and perhaps recopy the list if it looks too messy or scratched up. That's simple *editing*.

Publishing is when we share a piece of writing with its intended audience. In this case, the publishing is simple: hand the list to your spouse and send him or her off to the store. Or, hand it to your child with a couple of ten-dollar bills and keep your fingers crossed.

The effectiveness of your process will be evident in what comes home from the grocery store: either you will get what you want, or you will end up with a pile of junk food you never expected.

No One-Draft Wonders

You may not even be aware of it, but you have just used a writing process for this simplest of tasks. You planned what you were going to write, you drafted a note, then revised and edited it for another reader and maybe even published it. You went through a five-step process:

Pre-writing $\longrightarrow$ Drafting $\longrightarrow$ Revising $\longrightarrow$ Editing $\longrightarrow$ Publishing

The process of pre-writing, composing and revising writing is a natural one. Before writing, we make decisions about what we're going to write, why we're writing it and what form the writing is going to take. Next, we compose, or draft, the piece of writing. Then, good writers revise their work to ensure that the writing is clear and powerful. Most professional authors will tell you they revise a piece of writing a dozen times or more before it is published. Once the writing says what we want it to say, we make sure all the mechanics are in place and it is ready to share with an audience, a process known as editing. Not every piece of writing we do makes it to an audience – diaries and personal notes are often private – but even an e-mail is a kind of published writing. Publishing is that stage where our piece of print meets its readers.

Although a multi-stage process is common for most real-life writing, it has not always been the practice for most writing in school. In the past, much writing in school consisted of one-word or one-sentence responses to teacher-generated questions. It wasn't until the late 1970s that researchers such as Donald Graves began to pay attention to students' writing and to apply the processes that professional writers use to writing instruction. Since then, classroom researchers such as Nancie Atwell, Lucy Calkins and Shelley Harwayne have written about using the writing process with students of all ages. Now we teach students to pre-write, draft and revise their writing, then to edit for surface errors and finally to publish, or share it with an audience.

Most writers go through the processes we've just described, though it's rarely as simple as the five-step outline would indicate. Sometimes a writer will go back to his pre-writing plan several times, even during revision, and sometimes he may abandon a piece of writing altogether. The writing process varies from one writer to another and even one piece of writing to another.

The process of pre-writing, drafting, revising, editing and publishing is a good teaching tool, but is neither a formula nor a recipe for writing. The only simple truth is that good writing is *never* a one-draft wonder. Anyone who says, "I just sat down and wrote it," spent a lot of time planning and crafting in her head before the first word hit the page.

All this explains why the mechanical five-day writing plan (pre-writing on Monday, drafting on Tuesday, revising on Wednesday, editing on Thursday, publishing on Friday) contradicts what we know of a natural and effective writing process. Quite frankly, no one writes that way. As we'll explain later, real writing requires some flexibility in both time and process.

Pre-writing

Some journalists say that pre-writing takes up to 85 percent of their entire writing process.

Some writers maintain that the pre-writing stage is the most complex and time-consuming aspect of writing. A strong pre-writing plan makes the rest of the process easier and more efficient. Many decisions must be made before writing: what to write about, what form it will take, who might read it, and why they should.

The acronym RAFTS represents the decisions a writer must make before beginning: **R**ole-**A**udience-**F**ormat-**T**opic-**S**trong verb (or purpose for writing). **Role** is the perspective of the writer – a storyteller, an observer, a humorist, a person with a strong opinion, or most commonly, the writer herself. **Audience** refers to who will read the writing. Is the writing for other students, for the teacher, for the adult community? The tone and voice of the writing would vary for each of these audiences. **Format** describes the form the writing will take: essay, letter, memo, and so on. **Topic** is, of course, what the writing is all about. **Strong verb** describes the purpose of the writing: to inform, to entertain, to complain, to invite. (See the page 21 for a reproducible poster of RAFTS.)

Let's take a simple example. Suppose your students want to have pizza served in the cafeteria once a week. How does the RAFTS plan look?

Role: A group of students/customers with an opinion
Audience: The Principal and School Council
Format: A letter or petition
Topic: Addition to cafeteria menu
Strong verb: *Demanding* addition of pizza!

RAFTS can also provide useful guidelines for teachers when assigning writing topics or prompts. Effective writing prompts not only provide the writers with a topic and format, but also guide them in

Beyond Brainstorming

Brainstorming isn't the only way to get started. Here are seven other ways to start:

1. Talk the piece through.
2. Sketch the ideas in pictures or graphics.
3. Make an outline.
4. Take notes and organize them.
5. Use graphic organizers.
6. Respond to another piece of writing: get mad and get writing.
7. Pick key words out of the question or prompt.

knowing the purpose of their writing and whom the prospective reader might be. (See the RAFTS menu on page 22.)

For student writers, generating ideas can be the most difficult part of writing. It's a good thing for teachers to remember that the more students write, the easier it will be for them to think of something to write about. We find it's like writing out our annual holiday cards – we have trouble thinking of something to say to the person we correspond with only once a year, but never run out of things to tell the people we see every day!

Donald Graves, a pioneer in writing process instruction, stresses the importance of teaching our students to "see the world as a writer." As teachers, we should provide frequent demonstrations of our own ideas and everyday experiences that could be turned into writing pieces. We need to teach students to notice the things around them and keep track of their ideas in a writer's notebook. We should give them surveys and interest inventories to complete and store in their writing folders. We can show them how to get ideas from books they read. And, of course, we must always expose our students to a variety of writing genres to open up worlds of possibilities for authentic, purposeful writing.

Drafting

Drafting is the stage in which a writer puts his plan into action. The writer pours out his ideas on paper or on the computer in some semblance of sentences and paragraphs. The focus is getting ideas down; mechanics and spelling are not of primary concern at this stage. Advise students to spell and punctuate *as well as they can* and remind them that they can go back later to fix up errors. (Never send a message that spelling doesn't matter.) Emphasize that writing fluency matters here.

If your students are not accustomed to using temporary spelling, it may be necessary to model the process of stretching out words to hear all the sounds and using what they know about how letters go together. Similarly, while neat handwriting is not the first priority, students must be able to write legibly enough to read their own work later on.

In the same way, encourage students to paragraph as well as they can. Paul tells his students: "Paragraphing helps you organize your thoughts. It's probably the best invention in language in the last 400 years!" While the paragraphing of any piece will certainly change in revision, it's the best tool we have to give shape to thoughts as they flow into a piece of writing.

While your students are drafting or scribbling or crossing out (don't allow them to crumple up paper in despair – that's only in Hollywood movies) remind them to

- leave a space between each line (for revision later on)
- write on only one side of the paper
- write in pen (so drafting seems special and they don't waste time erasing)
- focus on getting ideas down on paper

- do the best they can – they'll fix the writing later

In any writing, the process of drafting is often mixed with that of revision. As they write, students will find themselves deleting, changing and crossing out. Occasionally they may get a new idea as they write. Even Paul, a classic linear-thinker, frequently digresses or develops new ideas as he works on a book.

The drafting stage is a convenient one for these random corrections and indirections, but too much crossing-out and pasting-over will bog down the writing. Paul's first rule for aspiring novelists is, "Finish it, then go back to fix it." He adds, "I never go back to the first sentence until I write the last one." There is some author hyperbole in this, but the truth remains: revising is best left for later on.

Revising

In writing, as in life, you don't have to be sick to get better.

As we demonstrated with the exercise at the beginning of this chapter, if someone else is going to read your writing, you will want to make sure that your ideas are stated as clearly as possible. The process of getting to clarity is revision.

Revision involves *adding, deleting, moving* or *changing* information to convey the message of the writing more effectively. Revision may take place at the word, sentence, paragraph or whole-text level. Sometimes revision may even mean starting over.

Teachers consistently complain that their students are unwilling to revise their work. No surprise – so are most professional writers, and they get paid for what they do. For student writers, the problem often stems from a lack of audience. If only the teacher is going to read a piece, why should they keep revising it over and over? So, the single most effective way to ensure that your students will improve their writing is to make sure they have a purpose and audience for their work. Whether your students are writing a note to the principal for permission to hold a school dance or writing a letter to their favorite author about her new book, they will want to write as persuasively and effectively as possible. Good revision will help them get their message across and achieve the results they want.

Keep reminding your students that reworking a piece of writing doesn't necessarily mean there is anything *wrong* with it. When they have to revisit an assignment in math or spelling, it's usually because the answers are incorrect or incomplete. Not so in writing. We need to convince our students that "you don't need to be sick to get better." Published writers are always striving to make good writing even better – more interesting, more effective, more powerful. So should your students.

Finally, look for ways to make revising less painful. Motivation wanes when students have to recopy an entire piece of writing for every revision. Obviously, drafting on the computer can help. But even handwritten copies can be revised by cutting out portions of text, adding in new sections, and changing what's there.

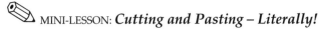 MINI-LESSON: *Cutting and Pasting – Literally!*

Model the revision process using a piece of your own writing. Copy a composition of about one page onto an overhead transparency. With pens, scissors and tape in hand, demonstrate to students how they can add, take away or change chunks of text without recopying the entire piece. Show them how to use carets (^) to add words, phrases or sentences. Model ways to add large sections of text, including taping another piece of paper onto the original draft. Demonstrate how to cut out sections of text with scissors or pen or by selecting a block of text on the computer. Let them see how they can make significant revisions to a draft without recopying the entire piece. Working this way gives a whole new meaning to the term "sloppy copy."

It's always easier to find – and correct – the flaws in someone else's writing. Near the end of most chapters, you will find student writing samples that may be duplicated for students to revise as they learn new elements of the writer's craft.

The use of computers in the writing process

Like most professional writers, Paul finds that computers have added stages to the writing process. "In the old days, we used to do a rough draft in pen. I'd type up a good draft on my faithful Underwood, then scribble over or physically cut and paste text. At the end, I'd pay a typist to make the whole thing presentable. These days, computers have made all that easier, but writers end up doing 10 or 12 drafts instead of three."

Computers offer many advantages to both students and teachers, especially at the revising stage. For kids, word processing makes it easy to revise and edit their work. For teachers, the ability to look at subsequent drafts permits us to observe a student's writing process. If the first and third drafts differ only by changes in spelling, we know that no meaningful revision has gone on.

Of course, before we expect students to draft on the computer, we'd better make sure they can keyboard quickly and efficiently. Slow hunt-and-peck typing impedes fluency and creativity and gets in the way of efficient writing and revision. It's unlikely that students in Grades 2 and 3 will be able to make reasonable use of computers for drafting; but by Grade 7 or 8, most kids can keyboard quite efficiently and will prefer to work directly on the computer.

The downside to computers, of course, is that kids often don't use them properly. Students should always save each draft with a new file number: Summervacation1, Summervacation2, Summervacation3, and so on. The advantage to the writer is that draft 3 is available if the computer crashes midway through draft 4. The advantage to teachers is that we can see if real revision is taking place. To paraphrase an adage, teach a child to write about her summer vacation and she's made it through one assignment; teach a child to revise her summer vacation essay and she's learned revision skills for the rest of her life.

A big reason why student writers are reluctant to revise a piece of writing is because they think it sounds just fine as it is. "I wouldn't have written it this way if I didn't think it was perfect" is their attitude. Because the writer knows what he *meant* to say, he may not realize that a reader may find parts of the text confusing. That's why it's important to build peer and teacher conferencing into the writing program. Often, someone else can point out a missing item or unclear points that the writer himself might miss.

Unfortunately, students often don't know how to respond to the work of another. That's why they end up using the conference to discuss spelling mistakes, or, worse, next weekend's basketball game. We suggest that you teach them a structured format for conferences: TAG.

Your Best Revision Tool: The TAG Conference

TAG Conference Sheets

Although TAG conferences should be conducted orally, there are times when the teacher may want the information written down for accountability. The "TAG Conference Sheet" on page 23 contains space for positive comments, questions, and advice, as well as the author's plans.

The acronym TAG stands for **T**ell something you like, **A**sk questions, **G**ive advice. The TAG structure is very effective for a number of reasons. First, it starts with the positive, reinforcing the writer's efforts and making her more receptive to constructive criticism that will follow. Second, when you ask questions, you are not criticizing the piece or passing judgment, you are simply indicating places that you, as a reader, find confusing or incomplete. Only in the last stage will you offer suggestions for the writer.

As with any new strategy, teachers must demonstrate the TAG process to help students understand how to respond to one another. Show them how to turn judgmental statements, such as "The ending doesn't make sense," into answer-prompting statements, such as "I don't understand why you brought your cat in at the end of the story."

It is essential to establish an atmosphere of trust in your classroom before your students will be comfortable sharing their writing and accepting feedback from others. Spend time working with the TAG process as a whole group, then provide opportunities for students to practise in pairs. We can't repeat this enough: **Students must have lots of time to practise a strategy before we expect them to use it on their own.** When students realize they will receive praise and support, as well as constructive commentary, most come around fairly quickly.

 MINI-LESSON: *Teaching the TAG Process*

1. Explain the process and model the kinds of comments that are appropriate at each stage of the conference. Remember that the focus is on the *writing*, not the *writer*.
2. Read a piece of your own writing aloud to the class (or use one of the student samples in this book). Ask the students to tell you something they liked about the piece of writing, to ask you some questions and to give you some advice. You may be surprised at the insights your students can provide for your own work.
3. Choose at least one thing to revise based on the student feedback. Ordinarily, a writer is under no obligation to make any of the recommended changes. However, in order to teach our students to make revisions, it's a good idea to require at least one revision in response to each TAG conference. Before ending your model conference, plan your next step using the "TAG Conference Sheet" on page 23. (If you have time, or are working with a computer and LCD projector, you may be able to make a revision right in front of your students' eyes.)
4. Ask for volunteers to read their writing aloud to the whole group and use the same process to respond to each of them. Model the kinds of comments that are appropriate at each stage of the process. In each

case, ask the writer to plan at least one revision to be made as a result of the conference.

5. Have students work in pairs to conference with one another as you circulate and listen to the responses. Take note of the kinds of comments you hear so you can share them with students as examples of good feedback. At the same time, be aware of difficulties arising so you can address them with the individuals as well as with the whole group.

Once this routine is well established, the TAG conference is an excellent addition to the writing program. It offers just what writers need: praise, specific feedback and ideas for improvement.

Editing

At some point, your students will be satisfied that their writing says just what they want it to say. They have focused their ideas and included details that support and enhance the main concept. They have organized the information logically and created an engaging lead and an effective conclusion. They have used the most powerful and precise words to convey the intended messages and create the needed images. Now it's time to clean up any errors in spelling and conventions before the writing is seen by an audience.

Many people tend to confuse or combine the processes of revision and editing, or neglect the revision component entirely. Even the terminology can be confusing. Some people consider editing to be the process of revising for meaning, while proofreading is the process of correcting surface errors. In the book business, "substantive editing" is the term used for major suggestions to the author; "copyediting" for the stage where minor errors and facts are checked before typesetting; and "proofing" for corrections just before the book is printed. Usually the substantive editor, copyeditor and proofreader are three different people.

No wonder kids get confused.

In most educational parlance (including this book), "editing" means correcting only the mechanics of the writing. It is not the time to jiggle paragraphs, add sentences or rework the ending; the editor's focus is entirely on spelling, grammar, punctuation and other mechanical issues.

Of course, experienced writers tend to undertake both revision and editing at the same time, for example, deleting an unnecessary apostrophe at the same time as fleshing out a missing detail. But for novice writers, it's a good idea to separate the two processes. After all, the more things a young writer must attend to, the less attention he is likely to pay to each. Wait until all the content is in place before focusing on mechanical details.

For some people, editing is even more difficult than revising. Because we're trained to read for meaning, we sometimes read what makes sense rather than what's really there. Reading out loud sometimes helps the reader focus on one word or sentence at a time. Starting at the end and reading backward helps the reader examine each word rather than the overall meaning of the text. Other proofreading hints may be found on page 24.

 MINI-LESSON: *The CUPS Strategy for Editing*

Student dictionaries, while useful for teaching, often don't contain the words student writers need help with spelling. Make sure there's a big, up-to-date dictionary in your writing corner for students to use as a reference.

CUPS is an acronym to remind students that when they edit, they should look for errors in **C**apitalization, **U**sage (grammar, correct word choice), **P**unctuation and **S**pelling. The CUPS poster on page 24 may be reproduced as an editing resource. If your students are not adept at editing for conventions, you may want to model the process by looking at one aspect at a time. Use a sample piece of writing and four different colors of editing pens to model the process. First, use one color to note any capitalization errors. Then skim through the text again, marking errors in word usage (grammar, verb tense, pronoun referents, etc.) with a different-colored pen. Go through a third time looking for missing or incorrect punctuation, and a fourth time noting and fixing spelling errors, each time with a different color.

Teach students to circle things that they aren't sure about so they can check them with a dictionary or someone who might know. As students become more adept at proofreading, they will be able to integrate fixing errors in capitalization, usage, punctuation and spelling all in the same process.

It's important to ensure that the students have access to a variety of resources such as dictionaries, lists of high frequency words and letter patterns, and thesauruses – and that they know how to use them.

The ability to find and correct one's own errors is an important skill. However, even the work of professional writers is subject to editorial scrutiny before being published. If your students' work is going to be put out for public scrutiny, do them a favor and take on the role of final editor. Not only does this help to ensure that their writing is error-free before publishing, it also lets you know the students' areas of difficulty in order to plan instruction.

Marking dozens of errors in a piece of student work for the student to go back and correct may improve the finished product, but it does little to improve either the writer's skill or her perception of herself as a writer. Don't waste your time adding dozens of red marks that will be ignored or thrown away. Instead, choose two or three key skills to use for teaching points. Sitting with the student while she painfully corrects dozens of errors is not a worthwhile use of your time or the student's.

Publishing

The last stage in the writing process is to produce a final copy that is neat, easy to read, and error-free. It would be wonderful if our students' work could be professionally printed, bound and published. But the reality of classroom "publishing" is simply sharing with an audience, whether it be reading the piece aloud to a friend, displaying it on the bulletin board, or printing it on the computer, complete with graphics

Journey to Publication

and title page. For students to see their work in print is exciting and motivational. The publishing stage of the writing process is what makes all the effort worthwhile. Other opportunities to publish student writing include these:

- word-processing, with formatting and graphics
- reading it out loud to the group
- sending letters to parents, newspapers, businesses, etc.
- displaying on permanent writing bulletin boards or in trophy cases
- creating a school newspaper, Web site or anthology
- adding to a personal coil-bound writing anthology
- binding, adding a card and placing it in the library

Remember that not all writing is intended for public consumption. Many of us study by jotting notes about key ideas. Math or science logs help learners clarify and organize their own thinking. Lists of words can help some people with spelling. Writing can also be a means of dealing with our thoughts and feelings. For example, a friend of Lori's was a principal in a small town where a murder took place. The community not only had to deal with mourning the deaths of their neighbors, but also to contend with the idea that their peaceful little town was not the safe haven they had grown to expect. Students and teachers in the school found it therapeutic to write about their thoughts, feelings and fears.

Although the most emotionally soothing work may be private writing, at other times of crisis, writers might be willing to share their ideas. Shelley Harwayne has edited a popular book of writings by students in New York City following the terrorist attacks of September 11, 2001. Not every group of students would choose to go public with their feelings on such an event. That choice – to go public or stay private – must be made by the writer and respected by the teacher.

Stages of the Writing Process

Pre-writing: *Getting Started*

- Decide what you're going to write about, why you're going to write it, what form it's going to take and who's going to read it.
- Use planning tools such as webs, charts and organizers to get your thoughts organized.
- Take time to think and talk to others.

Drafting: *Getting It Down*

- Think of drafting as putting your thoughts on the page.
- Compose as quickly as possible to get all your ideas down on paper.
- Write on only one side of the paper and leave a space between each line.

Revising: *Getting It Good*

- Make sure that your writing makes sense, that everything is in the right order, that all the important details are in place.
- Make sure that you've used the best and most interesting words and phrases.
- Make sure that you have a good beginning and ending.
- Make additions, deletions and changes for clarity and punch.

Editing: *Getting It Right*

- Check punctuation and capitalization.
- Check grammar and usage.
- Use a dictionary or spell-checker to correct spelling.
- Check for everything the computer won't catch – read your work out loud!

Publishing: *Getting It Out*

- Rewrite or print for display.
- Read your writing to an audience.
- Submit it to a publication or contest.

The RAFTS Framework

RAFTS is a useful reminder about decisions you have to make before drafting any piece of writing:

R – Role of the writer
Who is telling the story?

A – Audience
Who is going to be reading this?

F – Format
What form will the writing take – a letter, a diary, an essay, a story, a news report?

T – Topic
What is the main theme or idea of the writing?

S – Strong verb
What is the purpose for writing: to entertain, to amuse, to inform, to invite, to persuade?

RAFTS Menu

Choose one item from each column, then complete the sentence below:

Role	Audience	Format	Topic	Strong Verb
reporter	movie star	interview	scandal	inquiring
sports fan	hockey player	cartoon	big game	complaining
book character	boss	resumé	work experience	bragging
alien	Earthlings	poster	weather	whining
king/queen	subjects	announcement	new laws	proclaiming
Red Riding Hood	mourners	eulogy	the wolf	condemning
tooth fairy	dentist	letter	lost teeth	arguing
pioneer	family	diary	homestead	describing
cartoon character	audience	advertisement	new product	inviting
teacher	students	proclamation	messy desks	forbidding

As a (*role*) _____, write a (*format*) _____

for (*audience*) _____, (*strong verb*) _____

(*topic*) _____

TAG Conference Sheet

Writer's Name _____ Partner's Name _____

Title _____ Date _____

Tell something you like:

Ask questions (at least three):

Give advice:

Writer's Plan: (What am I going to do to improve this piece of writing?)

CUPS Strategy for Editing

Check your writing to make sure it passes the CUPS test:

C – Capital letters

U – Usage and grammar

P – Punctuation

S – Spelling

Eight Tips for Zestfully Clean Writing

Don't be embarrassed by how rough your rough drafts are. Clean them up. Follow Dr. Tim's eight tips for zestfully clean writing and polish up your work.

1. Don't proofread your writing right after you do the first draft. You're still too much in love with it. Take some time away from it and you'll be better able to see its faults.

2. Even though it might look goofy, read your work out loud. It helps you catch things you tend to skip over when you read silently. Even better, ask a friend to sit beside you and help you spot your errors.

3. Use a ruler. Not on your partner, on your paper! Hold it under each line as you read to focus on one line at a time.

4. Do things backwards. That's right. Start at the end and read to the beginning. When you do this, you pay attention to the way the words look, not the overall meaning.

5. Use a highlighter to mark words that you think may be wrong. Trust yourself. If a word looks wrong, it probably is.

6. When you find a wonky-looking word, try writing it again. Does the new version look write, I mean right?

7. Double trouble! We sometimes tend to make the same mistakes twice – or even more. So, once you know what kinds of mistakes you make, look for them when you proofread.

8. Make friends with the dictionary. It looks scarier than it is.

With thanks to Tim Caleval, assessment & evaluation consultant, Regina Board of Education

2

How Students Learn to Write – The Writing Workshop

Let's face it: most kids don't learn to write well from handing in writing that is simply graded and garbaged. They learn from receiving explicit instruction, by having many opportunities to write, by sharing and receiving feedback, and by revisiting their writing to improve it. Organizing all of that is up to you.

Elements of the Writing Workshop

The Writing Workshop is an organizational structure that enables the teacher to provide instructional supports for the class and still individualize the writing process for each student. Although the Writing Workshop may take a variety of forms, there are three basic elements: time, ownership and response.

Time

Good writing cannot be rushed. If we expect students to follow the writing process – to pre-write, draft, revise and edit – then we must allow them time to do so. In the same way, we cannot expect to teach a new genre each week. Effective instruction in the various genres of writing requires immersion in reading the form, careful teacher modeling and demonstration, and extensive guided practice. All this must be done before we ask students to apply their knowledge independently. It will probably take four to six weeks to thoroughly teach and practise writing in a particular genre. By this time, students should have completed several drafts of various pieces and taken at least one to publication.

Writers need extended and regular time frames in which to work. Scheduling the Writing Workshop for Thursdays from 1:00 to 1:30 p.m. will not be conducive to good writing. Some of your students will take that long to find their notebooks! Although we always have to be sensitive to the attention spans of our students, periods should be *at least* 40 minutes long and may extend well beyond an hour. We need to provide enough time for students to collect their thoughts, make decisions about

The **writing process** refers to the stages that a writer goes through as she plans, drafts, revises, edits and shares a piece of writing with an audience.

The **Writing Workshop** is an effective way to organize the writing program in your classroom.

what they are going to do, and give some sustained attention to the task at hand.

Ideally, students should be engaged in writing every day. Unfortunately, school life, with its assemblies, trips and special events, makes it difficult to find that writing time. At the very least, try to schedule the Writing Workshop two or three times a week. If too much time elapses between workshop sessions, students may lose interest in an ongoing writing project. Sometimes you might want to consider an intensive daily Writing Workshop for a few weeks at a time.

Regardless of your plan, consistency is important. Students should know when the Writing Workshop will be scheduled each week so they can be prepared for it.

Ownership

Ownership reflects the student's own role in making decisions about his or her writing process and product. It is human nature to be more engaged and more willing to expend effort in an activity that we have chosen ourselves. Writing is no exception. When students choose their topics, their genres, and their audiences, they are more likely to do their best work.

This reality doesn't mean that teacher-assigned writing has no place in the Writing Workshop. Sometimes we will want to assign writing tasks that teach a particular skill or strategy; sometimes we will require students to write in a certain genre or for a certain purpose. Teaching writing is a balance of instruction and the opportunity to write: a fine balance, indeed.

Whenever possible, we want to allow an element of choice and balance teacher assignments with opportunities for students to choose what they want to write. Even within the framework of a guided genre lesson, students should be given the opportunity to choose their topics or to choose which of several pieces they would like to take to publication. Fortunately, the nature of the Writing Workshop supports students working at different stages of the writing process at different times.

Response

Most writing, with the possible exception of diaries and journals, is meant to be read by someone else. Students need opportunities to share their writing with an audience – you, their peers, their parents, the local newspaper. They need and want feedback, both positive and constructive. This feedback is most effective when given *during* the writing process; indeed, research over many years has shown that grades and comments on a published piece of writing do little to improve a student's writing proficiency.

Often, the teacher is the first and most obvious audience for a student's writing, but if the writing is to be truly authentic, there must be other audiences too. Determining purpose and audience before writing helps writers to craft their words and motivates them to do their best.

Sample Schedule

Teaching
1:00–1:15
Writing and Conferencing
1:15–1:50
Sharing
1:50–2:00

Organizing the Writing Workshop

There is no single model for organizing and managing the Writing Workshop. Teachers structure their Writing Workshops in different ways according to the needs of their students and their own teaching styles. With younger students, Lori likes to do sustained Writing Workshop "units," scheduling 60-minute blocks almost every day for two to three weeks. Then she will ease up on writing to focus on another area of language arts, such as literature study. She finds this helps students maintain interest. Paul teaches writing to high school and university students, fitting his lessons and practice times into 75-minute blocks, sometimes (though not ideally) spaced a week apart, and requiring writing homework in between.

However we manage the time, most Writing Workshop sessions consist of four components: teaching, writing, conferencing (which takes place at the same scheduled time as writing) and sharing.

Teaching: 5–15 minutes

Lucy Calkins and others have written about the merits of brief, focused instruction, and we heartily agree. No television segment ever lasts more than 11 minutes, nor should any single lesson presentation if we want maximum effectiveness. Each mini-lesson should focus on one specific element of writing that the teacher has identified as a point of need for his students. Following the lesson, we should provide immediate opportunity for writing practice.

The mini-lesson may focus on a classroom *procedure* or routine, such as how to organize the writing folder or sign up for a conference. It might cover an aspect of *process*, such as a pre-writing or revising tool. It might deal with an aspect of *craft*, such as characterization or figurative language. Or it might focus on an aspect of *conventions*, such as where to put that pesky apostrophe.

Sometimes the mini-lesson will include a short writing task or require students to incorporate the skill into their existing writing. For example, if you've presented a lesson on strong verbs, you may want students to go back into an existing draft and highlight five verbs to make more vivid.

The point is this: keep your lessons short and sweet. Better to have more mini-lessons with follow-up than "brilliant" hour-long teaching extravaganzas which often exceed students' attention spans.

Writing and conferencing: 30–40 minutes

During writing time, students have three choices of what to do:

- Start a new piece of writing.
- Finish an incomplete piece.
- Go back and rework a completed draft.

By November, your students should have a collection of writing ideas in their folders that they can pick up and work on. The Writing Bingo game (see Chapter 4, page 63) is one way to develop this bank of ideas. Teacher Wilfred Burton keeps an ongoing class chart of writing ideas

Paul: I think it's time to talk about the merits of the short writing assignment.

Lori: I once heard a writer say he had never seen a piece of student writing in which the second 100 words were as good as the first.

Paul: So, why assign writing that's more than 100 words long?

Seize the teachable moment.

If a writing opportunity comes up during the school day, take advantage of it. Big news events, basketball victories or even snowball fights can make for powerful writing – even if they can't be planned ahead in your daybook.

Use the "honeybee" model for conferences – alight briefly at each student's desk for a progress report before moving on.

Lori: I'm really starting to question the value of peer editing for conventions. Sometimes the peer is no better at catching spelling mistakes than the writer!

Paul: And even if the peer is a good speller, is correcting someone else's work the best use of his or her time?

developed by the entire group. By the end of one year, his students had 112 ideas on the chart, ready for instant use by anyone in the room.

In writing, as with everything else, different people have different learning styles. For many of your students, writing is a social activity, which benefits from interaction and discussion. Others, however, will require quiet and privacy. Make sure your classroom arrangement makes allowances for different learning needs.

During writing time, you will usually be circulating among your students to conference with them, as needed. Your first priority should be students who seem to have writer's block. Help them get started before moving on to others.

On any given day, some students will be ready for revision and editing conferences. We suggest that you separate these two types of conferences, so that young writers can focus on clarity and effectiveness of content before correcting conventions. These conferences, which will be longer than just a few minutes, require some preparation on your part. You may want to have two baskets, one labeled "Revision Conferences" and the other "Editing Conferences." When students are ready for a conference, they simply place their writing piece in the appropriate basket. You can then review the piece of writing as you have time to prepare an appropriate response.

Peer conferencing can be a valuable experience for both partners, but it must be carefully structured. A conversation about last night's hockey game isn't going to make either student a better writer. Model, demonstrate and practise making appropriate responses, focusing on content and style, so that students know how to conduct themselves in a peer conference and what their responsibilities are. The TAG strategy, described on pages 16–17, is an excellent way to structure effective peer conferences.

Keep a record of which students you've conferenced with and what you've discussed. You might want to ask students to maintain a list of things they have learned in the front of their writing portfolios or notebooks.

Sharing: 5–10 minutes

Sharing time is an effective way to wrap up the Writing Workshop. It brings everyone back together to reflect and celebrate. Some teachers have a special Author's Chair in the classroom for this very purpose. One or two students are invited to share their writing and often there is a sheet for them to "sign up" to read. Unless the writer has specifically requested help with an aspect of the writing, do not make this a time for constructive feedback, but for listening and celebrating.

Frequently Asked Questions

The balance of this chapter answers questions that many teachers pose about organizing the Writing Workshop. You may find this section a helpful summary.

Materials needed for the
Writing Workshop:

- something to write *with*
- something to write *on*
- something to store writing *in*

Do I need special materials or equipment for the Writing Workshop?

Basically, all you need to start the Writing Workshop are something to write *with* and something to write *on*. Each student should also have a means of storing his or her writing, whether it be a folder, three-ring binder or notebook. A tri-fold portfolio can help students organize their writing into categories such as "Writing Ideas," "Works-in-Progress" and "Finished Drafts." Writing portfolios are available commercially, but students can create their own writing folders using large sheets of bristol board. For students who have trouble keeping track of loose sheets of paper, a notebook or binder might be preferable.

You will also want to establish procedures for storing these items. Lori teaches her students to file their writing folders alphabetically in a plastic crate. Paul expects his students' computer files to be saved by draft: 1, 2, 3, and so on.

As you establish the routines that work for you and your students, you will add equipment and materials. You might designate a particular space or table for conferencing or for editing. Some teachers like to decorate a plastic lawn chair to be used exclusively as an Author's Chair. You will surely want to have a supply of dictionaries, visual dictionaries, thesauruses and other reference tools, including classroom charts and posters.

Don't forget the importance of your classroom library and magazine rack. The more we ask students to write in different genres, the more we have to supply them with models of professional writing.

How do I get the Writing Workshop started?

Every teacher organizes the workshop in a unique way and you will have to find the routines that suit you and your students best. With those caveats in mind, here is the routine that Lori uses to initiate her Writing Workshop.

Week 1: Make or distribute writing folders or other organizers. Spend at least two class periods just on idea-generating and pre-writing activities from the genre of your choice. (Many ideas are found in subsequent chapters.) By this time, your students should have a cache of writing ideas and at least three pre-writing plans from which to choose. Start each session with a mini-lesson and end with an opportunity to share. Invite each student to share one great idea – and encourage the rest to add new ideas to their lists.

Week 2: Have students choose one of their plans to turn into a draft. (The other materials should stay in their writing folders.) Use one of your own models to demonstrate to students how to compose a first draft. Take another class period to repeat the drafting process. You don't want these to be long compositions – one page is plenty. Students should have at least two drafts to work with by the end of Week 2. Quicker writers can write more drafts. Begin to encourage independent pacing. End each session with "Author's Chair," where a couple of students volunteer to share their drafts.

Week 3: By now, all of your students should have at least two drafts in their writing folders. Have them choose one to revise and rework for publication. Introduce TAG conferences and practise them as a group. Then have students work in pairs to hold peer conferences on their drafts. Each student must make at least one meaningful revision to his original draft; of course, more than one would be even better. Model the cut-and-paste procedure (either on paper or on the computer) so drafts don't have to be recopied.

Week 4: When the students have completed their revisions, teach the CUPS editing process. If we want the students to publish their writing pieces, we should take them in for a final edit. Ask them to word-process or recopy the writing, and, voilà, you've gone through the whole writing process. While you might want to walk students through this process once in a while, for specific purposes, most of them should now be able to undertake the steps independently.

What do I do with the student who won't stay on task?

What do you do with her during math class? or during social studies? Chances are, the student who can't function independently in the Writing Workshop is the same one who can't function independently in any other classroom situation. Effective classroom management is essential in all subject areas.

A key to classroom management is to make sure that you have set out your expectations clearly. Introduce the routines and procedures one at a time. As we emphasized earlier, give time to practise before expecting students to function independently.

One important routine involves what to do if a student needs help and the teacher is unavailable. The answer is simple: students should seek help from another student first. Therefore, you will have to teach *all* the students how to ask for help as well as how to respond. If it is quiet writing time, or the teacher is unavailable, a simple routine is for the student to place a yellow card on the corner of the desk, and move on to another project until the teacher is free.

Although the Writing Workshop is designed to offer students choice, those choices should be carefully monitored. You will want to watch the students' daily progress and deal with specific situations that arise. It's always a good idea to keep an anecdotal record of daily events, both for marking and for planning instruction.

You may want to consider setting up contracts for so much writing per day for those students who are unable to set their own goals. A last resort would be to remove a student from the workshop setting to work on her own until she can function within the group. Banishment has been an effective punishment for many years, from Socrates in ancient Greece to little Johnny Blowhard acting up in your classroom.

Both Paul and Lori have found that many of their weakest students respond best to the workshop environment. Behavior problems often arise when students find the work too difficult; in the Writing Workshop, students are motivated by success and choice.

Don't forget the parents!

Parents can be your best allies for the Writing Workshop, but only if you bring them on side. Send home some ideas on how they can help.

- Tell them what genre you're working on.
- Explain how and when to edit their child's work.
- Say when you might need help in publishing.
- Provide calendars for project due dates.
- Share rubrics for expectations and marking.
- Outline how to do a TAG conference at home.

How do I keep track of everyone when they're all at different stages and working on different projects?

Different teachers use different systems for monitoring their students. Because your students will be working on different projects in various stages, you might want to conduct a quick roll call, known as "Status of the Class." You simply take a class list and create a code for each stage of the writing process: Pre, D, R, E, Pub. As you call out each student's name, mark the stage he is working on. Or, use the form on page 34 to track the progress of a particular piece. You can ask the kids to sign up on the chart themselves. With younger students, you might use a pocket chart and file cards with different colors for the five stages. Whatever way you choose to record "Status of the Class," you'll encourage your students to follow the process and use their time effectively. Moreover, you'll have a way to monitor their progress, which is important for both instruction and evaluation.

Another option is for students to keep an ongoing writing log (see page 35) in their writing folders. At the beginning of each session, the student notes what she is planning to work on and at the end of each session, what she accomplished. This procedure encourages students to set goals and self-monitor. The teacher will want to check these logs regularly to monitor progress and to evaluate.

How do I organize small-group activities?

The Writing Workshop lends itself perfectly to differentiated instruction. Students work at individual rates on individual projects. However, there are times when students will need to work in pairs or in small groups for conferencing or instruction.

If your students are not accustomed to working in groups, you will need to develop some procedures and behavior norms. Establish routines for moving desks into twos, threes or fours quickly and efficiently. As always, practise first so the arrangement can be quick and automatic when you need it.

Another issue is how to create pairs for peer conferences. Lori avoids the social issues that arise over partnering in this way: when someone is ready for a peer conference, he simply writes his name in the box drawn on the chalkboard. The next person who is available or ready for a conference erases the first person's name and joins him for a conference. Then the box is free for someone else to sign in. No one else can have a conference while someone's name is in the box. If a child doesn't want to conference with that person, she will have to wait until the box is empty. Obviously, Lori keeps an eye on the box to make sure that one name doesn't remain too long; in that case, she might assign someone to do the conference or do it herself.

When should students be able to use the computer?

There's no sense using a computer for writing until students are skilled enough in keyboarding that it doesn't slow them down. A lot of kids waste a great deal of time making fancy title pages that teach them little about graphics and nothing about writing.

Always be ready for the line "My computer crashed!" Computers do, of course, but not nearly as often as students would like to have you think. Even if the computer crashes in printing the finished piece, a student should have paper drafts or files ready to turn in on time.

By Grade 4 or 5, most students will be able to publish some of their work by word-processing the edited draft. By Grades 7 and 8, many students will be drafting directly on their computers at home or in school. Be sure, at that point, that you get to see each draft. Often a complete set of files at the various stages, submitted by e-mail or on disc, is more useful than a printed final draft.

The great majority of your students will have access to some kind of computer at home. Nonetheless, if you're going to ask for work to be done on a computer, you must provide access to one in your room or elsewhere in the school for students who are not so fortunate.

The Internet is often useful for researching topics, though care must be taken with the reliability of the Web sites used. Older students can store the information they find on personal discs; younger students will want to use up tons of your paper. It may be best to limit research to five printed sheets, or risk the wrath of your School District's business administrator.

How do I evaluate the Writing Workshop?

We don't evaluate the Writing Workshop; we evaluate students' progress toward their learning goals. So, consider what you want your students to know and be able to do each term. Evaluating their progress toward those goals will guide your instruction and provide grades for reporting.

Assuming that using the writing process is one of your learning objectives for students, you will want to assess process as well as product. Anecdotal notes, "Status of the Class" charts, TAG conference sheets, and learning logs will all provide useful information about your students' progress.

When evaluating the students' writing products, you will want to consider the quality of the message and the craft as well as basic conventions. The Six Traits rubrics in Chapter 3 will provide you with valuable tools for ongoing evaluation and coaching as well as numbers for grading.

Students need to understand that quality supersedes quantity in writing. We suggest three drafts and one published piece for each genre unit. The published piece should include a pre-writing plan, at least two drafts with evidence of revision, and a polished final copy. Don't settle for less.

Status of the Class

Dates

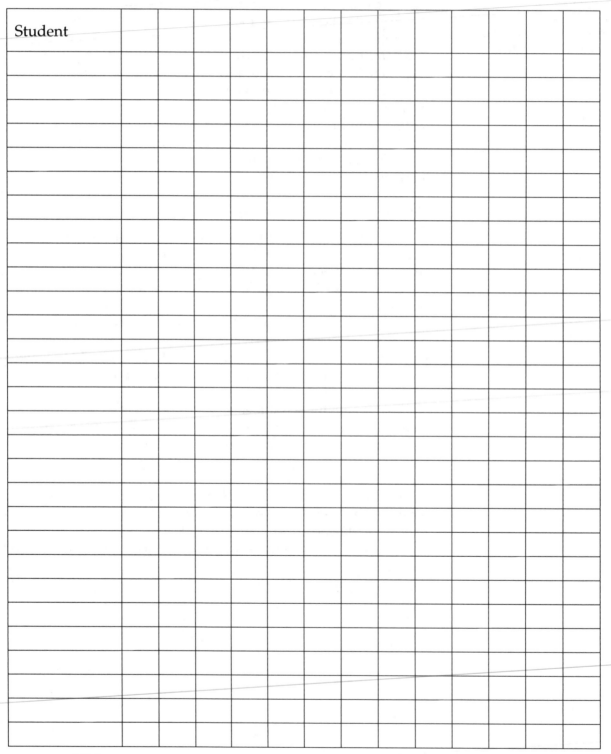

Student															

P = Pre-writing; D = Drafting; R = Revising; E = Editing; H = Publication; A = Absent from class; O = Other activity

My Writing Log

Name _____

Date	What I plan to do today	What I accomplished today

3

Using Rubrics for Writing Instruction and Assessment – The Six Traits

Most of us can't begin to count the hours we've spent grading and correcting student writing. Often we labor over marking various kinds of corrections and suggesting improvements, only to have kids ignore our feedback and focus on their mark. Research tells us that grades and comments on final drafts have little impact on improving student writing. So, what can we do to ensure that the time and energy expended on writing assessment helps to make our students better writers?

The answer is to provide specific comments during the writing process, when students still have an opportunity to do something with their writing. We know that student writing improves significantly when students are provided with clear criteria for success and opportunities to revise their work based on these criteria.

All too often, we have a sense of what "good" writing is, but can't always articulate what makes the writing "good" – or what needs to be done to improve it. This is where the Six Traits come in. The Six Traits rubrics give teachers and kids a language to discuss writing. By focusing on specific criteria, we get a common set of expectations. It not only takes the mystery out of assessment for students, it also makes evaluation easier and more consistent for teachers.

In this chapter, we've provided a set of rubrics based on the Six Traits that describe each criterion at different levels of proficiency. These levels are indicated by the numbers 5, 4, 3, 2 and 1, with 5 representing the highest level of proficiency. Using the traits and the rubrics, both teachers and students can identify where a piece of writing fits on the continuum and what needs to be done to improve it.

What Makes "Good" Writing?

What are the criteria for good writing? Your students will be the first to tell you that no two teachers have the same set of expectations. In a classic study by Paul Diederich, 53 people from different walks of life were asked to score a set of 300 papers on a scale of one to nine, based

Lori has had success with teaching students as young as Grade 3 to score writing samples according to the Six Traits rubrics.

on their own standards of effective writing. Amazingly, no paper received fewer than five different scores and a third of the papers received every score from one to nine!

But in analyzing the thousands of responses made by the scorers, Diederich and his colleagues found that all the comments fit into only five categories. Diederich's categories were *ideas* (relevance, clarity, development), *form* (organization), *flavor* (style, interest, sincerity), *mechanics* (grammar, punctuation, spelling), and *wording and phrasing* (choice and arrangement of words).

In the 1980s, Diederich's seminal work on writing criteria was extended. A group of teachers from the Beaverton School District in Oregon worked with researchers from the North West Regional Educational Laboratories to define the elements of effective writing and build rubrics for teacher and student use. These elements, known as the Six Traits, are now used in classrooms around the world. They can be summarized as follows: *ideas and content, organization, voice, word choice, sentence fluency* and *conventions*. (In some contexts, presentation is included as a separate element, too.)

We'll be covering ways to teach these traits throughout the book. In this chapter, we'll provide an overview of the traits so you and your students can develop a common language to talk about good writing. ·

Ideas and Content

This trait examines the overall theme of the piece of writing. Does it have a main idea? Is the idea focused? Does the writing include effective details that support the main idea? Ruth Culham suggests that this trait is best developed through four stages: (1) choosing an idea, (2) narrowing it down and focusing, (3) elaborating on it, and (4) adding strong details to support and enhance the main idea. We'll be showing how to do that in the next chapter on personal memoir.

Rubric for Ideas and Content: *Main idea, supporting details, focus and theme*

5	Fresh, original treatment of ideas; well-developed theme from start to finish, with relevant, strong supporting detail
4	Clear, focused, interesting ideas with appropriate details that enhance the main idea
3	Evident main idea with some supporting details; may lack focus or contain bits of irrelevant material or gaps in needed information
2	Some attempt at support, but main theme may be too general or confused by irrelevant details.
1	Writing lacks a central idea; development is minimal or non-existent.

Organization

Organization is about the logical and effective presentation of ideas and details. Good organization keeps a piece of writing together and makes it easy for the reader to follow. It involves "hooking" the reader with an engaging lead and wrapping up the piece with a satisfying conclusion. The organizational structure of a piece will depend on the purpose for writing; for example, a recipe is organized in a different way than an editorial. Teaching students about different genres and text forms will help them learn to organize their writing in ways that are appropriate to the topic and purpose.

Rubric for Organization: *Structure, unity, lead and conclusion*

5	Effectively organized in a logical and creative way; has a unique and engaging introduction and conclusion
4	Structure moves the reader smoothly through the text; well organized with an inviting introduction and a satisfying closure
3	Organization is appropriate, but conventional. There is an obvious attempt at an introduction and conclusion.
2	An effort has been made to organize the piece, but it may be a "list" of events. The introduction and conclusion are not well developed.
1	A lack of structure makes this piece hard to follow. Lead and conclusion may be weak or non-existent.

Voice

Voice has been called "the fingerprints of the writer on the page." It can be the hardest trait to define, but the easiest to recognize. Voice is a combination of feeling, style and connection to the audience. It makes a piece of writing distinctive and engaging. It may convey satire, humor, anger, or sadness – depending on the author's purpose and whom he is writing for.

While voice in first-person writing is easier to identify, every piece of third-person writing also has a voice. Read some of Bill Bryson's *A Short History of Nearly Everything* and you can "hear" the author as much as you would in his first-person travel books. As teachers, we can help our students put voice into their writing by teaching them how to give their writing a tone for a specific audience.

Rubric for Voice: *Energy, personality and sense of audience*

5	Passionate, compelling, energetic; shows emotions such as humor, honesty, pathos, suspense or liveliness; strong sense of audience and purpose
4	Expressive, engaging, sincere tone that speaks to the reader. The writer behind the words comes through clearly.
3	Voice is generally appropriate to audience and purpose. Tone is pleasant, but not distinctive; may have "sparks" of interest or emotion.
2	Voice may be mechanical or erratic. The writer seems to lack a sense of audience.
1	Writing tends to be flat or lifeless. Style does not suit audience or purpose.

Word Choice

Word choice refers to the language a writer uses to express his or her ideas. Effective words are not just descriptive; they are precise. They are carefully chosen to convey the intended message clearly and create pictures in the reader's mind. One of the best ways to teach word choice is to engage students in reading that enriches their vocabularies and shows how effective language can be.

Rubric for Word Choice: *Precision, clarity, effectiveness and imagery*

5	Carefully chosen words convey strong, fresh, vivid images consistently throughout the piece.
4	Word choice is functional and appropriate. The writer has made some attempt at description, which sometimes may seem overdone.
3	Words are likely to be correct, but lack flair. The writer may overuse generalized words and modifiers.
2	Word choice is monotonous; may be repetitious or immature. The writer uses patterns of conversation rather than book language.
1	Vocabulary range is limited and may be inappropriate.

Sentence Fluency

Sentence fluency refers to the way the text *sounds* more than what it *means*. Fluency is achieved by varying the lengths, types and structures of sentences. Short sentences are used for emphasis. Long, nuanced sentences are used for rhythm and imagery. Balanced sentences are used to carefully explicate ideas. The result is writing that has an almost musical cadence; it is a pleasure to read such text aloud.

Rubric for Sentence Fluency: *Rhythm, tone and variety*

5	High degree of craftsmanship in sentence length and form; the writing sounds rhythmical to read aloud.
4	Easy flow and rhythm to most of the piece; good variety in sentence length and structure
3	The writer is generally in control of sentence structure, but sentences often follow a similar structure without much variation for effect.
2	Generally in control, but lacking variety in length and structure
1	No "sentence sense"; run-on or choppy sentences predominate.

Conventions

"Over 50 years of research confirms that grammar exercises in isolation do not improve student writing."
– George Hillocks, 1994

Conventions are the mechanics of writing: spelling, punctuation, capitalization and grammar. Australian author Mem Fox describes conventions as the "good table manners" of written language. Often children (and teachers) become too focused on conventions in their writing process. In truth, computer spell-checkers and grammar-checkers are restoring this trait to its proper place in the editorial lineup: dead last.

Nonetheless, our students need to know the standard conventions of English for fear of having their ideas dismissed due to a misspelled word or a misplaced comma. Mini-lessons and individual conferences as part of the Writing Workshop are the most effective way to teach conventions. Although some publishers sell worksheets to cover these issues, such disconnected drills have little effect on real writing. Better to devise a focused lesson based on the specific needs of your students. Page 46 provides a reminder of the conventions most students will know at various grade levels.

Rubric for Conventions: *Spelling, grammar, punctuation and capitalization*

5	The paper contains few, if any errors in conventions. The writer shows control over a wide range of conventions beyond grade-level expectations. Some errors may result from experimentation with words and sentences.
4	The writer shows strong control of conventions. Writing is generally correct, but may be risk-free.
3	Occasional errors are noticeable, but minor. The writer uses conventions with enough skill to make the paper easily readable.
2	More frequent errors, inappropriate to the grade level, are evident but the reader can still follow the piece.
1	Errors in conventions make the writing difficult to follow. The writer seems to know some conventions, but confuses many more.

How to Use the Six Traits Rubrics

The rubrics on the preceding pages can be used for both assessment and instruction in all genres of writing. If we plot a piece of writing on a rubric – or on all six rubrics – it helps us identify the strengths and determine where the writing needs to go next. The rubric provides us with the language to talk to student writers about their writing and to guide them to higher levels of proficiency. Research tells us that when students have opportunities to revise their writing based on specific and focused feedback, the quality of writing improves significantly. These rubrics *may* be used for grading, but are most useful during the revision stages of the writing process.

The same rubrics, worded in language that students can readily understand (see pages 42 to 44), can guide students in evaluating and monitoring their own writing. When George Hillocks reviewed the research on student self-evaluation using rubrics, he concluded that this practice leads not only to more effective revisions, but also to superior first drafts.

Ideally, teachers and students should work together to build their own rubrics. When students have "ownership" of the process, they are more likely to comply with the criteria. They understand both the language and the intent.

A Possible Marking Scheme

Process: 20 marks
using anecdotal
records, checklists,
TAG Conference
Sheets
Product: 30 marks
using the Six Traits
rubrics
*Double the score to get a
percentage total.*

Evaluating student writing

We emphatically recommend that grades for student writing should combine both process and product. The final piece of writing is only one piece of the overall learning that should be evaluated. Participation in the writing process and progress over time should figure significantly in a student's grade. Assessment on a particular trait, or on all six traits, is only a part of how you should evaluate student work.

Nonetheless, the one-page rubric on page 45 may be used to obtain a mark as well as provide instant feedback for the writer. Simply allocate a score from 1–5 for each trait and total them to obtain a score out of 30.

Ideas for teaching each of the Six Traits are found throughout this book, as we apply the elements of effective writing to specific genres. Be sure to focus on one trait at a time, discussing the elements of the rubric and linking it to what students are actually writing. Use some of the writing samples provided in this book or materials you have collected from previous years for students to practise scoring based on the five-point scale. Then have students work in pairs or in small groups to revise the writing to improve that particular trait. As we said earlier, it's always easier to see (and improve upon) the flaws in someone else's writing than in your own. Once students are comfortable with using the rubrics on "other kids'" work, you can guide them to assess and revise their own writing.

The Six Traits Rubrics for Students

Rubric for Ideas

5	The main idea of my paper comes through clearly. My paper is full of interesting, unique details that hold the reader's attention.
4	My paper makes sense. The main idea is clear. My paper contains many interesting details.
3	The reader can tell what my main idea is. My writing contains some interesting details, but it could use more. Sometimes, there is information that I don't really need.
2	It's hard to figure out what my main idea is. I just wrote whatever I could think of on the topic.
1	I'm not even sure what my main idea is. I just wrote whatever came into my head.

Rubric for Organization

5	My writing is organized in a way that is creative and easy to follow. My lead grabs the reader's attention and the conclusion wraps the piece up just right.
4	My organizational plan works well to keep the writing clear. The lead hooks the reader's attention and the conclusion is solid.
3	This paper is quite easy to follow from beginning to middle to end. I've tried to write a lead and a conclusion.
2	I tried to follow a plan, but I think my writing wanders a little. I have a lead and conclusion, but I'm not totally happy with them.
1	My paper is hard to follow. I wrote about too many things. The paper just starts without any kind of hook and ends suddenly.

The Six Traits Rubrics for Students *continued*

Rubric for Voice

5	My writing is full of enthusiasm and energy. I love the sound of the voice and I think readers will love it too.
4	My writing sounds lively. I think a reader will enjoy reading it.
3	My writing sounds okay. Some parts have a little flair.
2	I'm not sure whether this writing sounds like me or not. I don't know whether a reader would find it interesting.
1	I don't think my writing has much personality.

Rubric for Word Choice

5	I have thought about every word to make my meaning clear and paint a picture in the reader's mind.
4	I have used colorful, vivid words here and there.
3	I didn't think much about the words I chose. I guess some of them are cool.
2	I don't really have any interesting words in my writing. I just put down whatever words came to my mind to tell the story.
1	I don't even have a picture in my mind of what I'm talking about. The words I use are good enough, aren't they?

The Six Traits Rubrics for Students

Rubric for Sentence Fluency

5	My writing is clear and smooth from start to finish. My sentences are different lengths and begin in many different ways. This piece sounds good to read out loud.
4	My writing is rhythmical and smooth most of the time. Most of my sentences begin in different ways. I've used some short and long sentences for effect.
3	My writing is smooth and clear in most places. Many of my sentences are similar, but I've tried to vary some of them.
2	A lot of my writing needs smoothing out. Some sentences could go together and some need to be cut in two. I didn't really think much about changing my sentences.
1	My writing sounds choppy or boring when I read it out loud. Some of the sentences are too long.

Rubric for Conventions

5	I have checked over my spelling and punctuation and I think that they are excellent. You will have trouble finding any mistakes in my work. I paid careful attention to conventions to make sure my writing is clear.
4	You won't find many errors in this paper, except maybe in very hard words. I understand how conventions make my writing clear and I paid attention to them.
3	This paper may have a few errors, but I checked it over quite carefully. My message is clear, I think.
2	I might have quite a few errors in this piece. I'm not too good at catching my own mistakes. I hope my message is clear enough.
1	There are lots of mistakes in this piece and I'm afraid it might be a little difficult for a reader to understand.

Scoring Rubric for Writing

Based on "Six Traits" Analytic Assessment Scoring Guide and Regina Public Schools' Rubric for Writing Assessment

	5 Exemplary	4 Strong	3 Satisfactory	2 Developing	1 Below Expectations
Ideas/Content	fresh, original treatment of ideas; well-developed theme with relevant and engaging detail	clear and focused; appropriate details enhance the main idea.	evident main idea with some support; may be somewhat mundane	some attempt at support or expansion, but main theme may be too general or confused by irrelevant detail.	Writing may lack a central idea; development is minimal or non-existent.
Organization	effectively organized in logical and creative manner; engaging introduction and conclusion	order or structure moves the reader smoothly through the text; inviting introduction and satisfying closure	Organization is appropriate but conventional; obvious attempt at lead and conclusion	some evidence of organizational plan; may be a list of events; introduction and/or conclusion are not well developed.	Writing lacks clear sense of direction; may be ideas strung together loosely; ineffective or non-existent lead and closure
Voice	individual and engaging; strong sense of audience and purpose	sincere and engaging; recognizes audience	pleasant tone; some personality and style evident; voice generally appropriate	Voice may be erratic or non-existent; lacks sense of audience	flat, lifeless
Word choice	powerful and engaging words, carefully selected to convey the intended impression in a precise, interesting and natural way	broad range of vocabulary; uses colorful language, but it may be overdone	Words are adequate and correct, but lack flair and originality.	no evidence of precision or description; may be immature; may be "stream of consciousness" thinking	limited vocabulary range
Sentence fluency	Well-crafted sentences with varied length and structure create a rhythmical flow to the text.	Writing flows easily, with good variety in sentence length and construction.	many similar structures; occasional effort at variety and fluency	generally in control, but lacks variety in sentence length and construction	choppy sentences; most are short and simple in structure or rambling.
Conventions	Writer demonstrates a mastery of standard writing conventions beyond grade-level expectations; some errors may result from experimentation.	Writer demonstrates strong control of conventions; writing is generally correct, but may be risk-free.	reasonable control over conventions; may have occasional errors	There are frequent errors in conventions, but they do not interfere with readability of the piece.	Numerous errors in conventions may interfere with reading.

Used with permission of Regina Public Schools

A Grade-Level Guide to Conventions

Grade	Spelling	Caps	Punctuation	Grammar/ Usage	Paragraphs
3	• spells grade-level words appropriately in final draft • experiments with expanded vocabulary	• names, I, titles, holidays, greeting and closing of letters	• commas for day/month/year • apostrophes in contractions • periods for abbreviations	• simple sentences • irregular plurals	
4	• spells grade-level words and many expanded vocabulary words appropriately in final draft • may confuse homophones	• uses caps correctly in final draft	• commas for words in a series • quotation marks • apostrophes in sing. possessive • knows and applies rules for quotation marks	• complete sentences • correct verb tense	• begins to use paragraphs
5/6		• uses caps correctly in outlines	• commas in complex sentences, separating clauses • quotation marks • plural possessives	• writes complete sentences using appropriate forms of irregular verbs • uses adjectives and adverbs correctly	• writes in paragraphs • includes topic sentences in expository paragraphs
7/8		• uses correct capitalization consistently	• uses some complex punctuation: colons, semicolons, hyphens, etc.	• uses effective transitions, including pronoun referents; combines sentences using conjunctions	• uses paragraphs correctly

4

Telling Their Own Story – The Personal Memoir

Here's a personal memoir that Lori wrote as a model for her students. Not even the names have been changed to protect the innocent.

"Don't go near the pond!" were my aunt's parting words as Julie and I left the house. For two ten-year-olds, this was more an invitation than a warning. Careful to avoid my aunt's watchful eye as she stood at the kitchen window, we headed straight for the pond.

On the bank of the great sea, our galleon awaited. Actually, the galleon was just an old door, and the sea little more than a stagnant pond where cows and other four-legged creatures came to drink. But for two prairie kids, this was our passport to adventure.

We hopped on the door and poled across the murky water with a broom handle. We kept a wary eye out for pirates, sea-monsters and my sometimes-vigilant aunt. But halfway across the pond, our waterlogged door began to sink. The water covered our toes, crept to our ankles and began to climb to our knees. There was only one thing to do.

We took a deep breath, plugged our noses and jumped!

Fortunately, the water of our great sea wasn't too deep. We made it to the shore safely, the only casualty our soaking wet jeans. But how could we get past my aunt in these dripping denims?

Surely, we thought, the cool October breeze would dry them in no time. We climbed into the nearby treehouse, stripped off our pants and hung them in the tree. Then we sat, waiting for them to dry. And waited. And waited. When my aunt called us in for dinner, the jeans were mostly dry but we were chilled to the bone.

If my aunt had seen our jeans flapping in the wind, she never said a word. She must have figured that an afternoon spent shivering in our skivvies was enough punishment for two ten-year-old adventurers.

Lori's story is an example of the personal memoir, sometimes called a recount or personal narrative. Unlike the short story, a personal memoir does not always have a plot, but is organized around a central theme or idea that is revealed through a sequence of events. Though there may be creative exceptions, the memoir is usually based on an experience of the writer. The purpose of this genre is obvious: to entertain the reader and to capture the flavor of something that really happened.

We suggest beginning the year with the personal memoir for two reasons: reading the memoirs will help you learn about your students and it's fairly easy for writers to come up with material. While we'd like to think older children are somewhat less focused on themselves than Kindergarten students, even adolescents frequently return to that great literary theme: me, me, me. The personal memoir helps to give shape to that classic theme and teaches valuable writing skills that will be useful throughout the year.

Personal memoirs are generally based on events that happened to the writer – the truth "with stretchers," as Mark Twain would say. Sometimes a personal memoir will take the form of an observational story, such as a newspaper report or a biographical sketch. Some memoirs are descriptions of events that happened to others, often with details added to improve the retelling, and some, including the 2002 Newbery Award winner *A Single Shard*, are fictional accounts. Many popular books are recounts: for example, Eve Bunting's *Smoky Night* describes a child's reaction to the Los Angeles riots and *The Diary of Anne Frank* recounts a Jewish girl's experience hiding from the Nazis.

PERSONAL MEMOIR FRAMEWORK

Purpose	Organization
To tell about an event or series of events	The structure is based on the passage of time and a sequence of events. BEGINNING: Provides the reader with any necessary information about who, what, when, where, why MIDDLE: Outlines an event or series of events presented in chronological order END: May provide a summary or personal reaction

Language Features

✳ Generally told in the past tense
✳ Often told in the first person
✳ Has many action verbs
✳ Features specific characters who participated in the event
✳ Uses transition words to give indication of time or order
✳ Evokes the five senses through description
✳ Reveals feelings of the author
✳ May use dialogue to reveal characters and move the story along

Forms

Diary, personal memoir of an event, autobiography, newspaper article, biographical sketch, story, picture book, Web site or PowerPoint presentation

Reader's Digest and the Chicken Soup books are not only great sources of personal memoirs, they sometimes publish works written by students and other non-professional writers.

Immerse Students in the Genre

Much of the material we read in school, whether for student reading or teacher read-aloud, is in the personal narrative genre. It's important to provide students with a variety of examples so that they can read and hear the various forms that are possible within this genre. You will find some student examples at the end of this chapter. The list below features read-aloud picture books in the recount form which should appeal to students of all ages:

> *Owl Moon* by Jane Yolen
> *Harvey Slumfenburger's Christmas Present* by John Burningham
> *Smoky Night* by Eve Bunting
> *Something Beautiful* by Sharon Wyeth
> *Wilfrid Gordon McDonald Partridge* by Mem Fox
> *The Day Jimmy's Boa Ate the Wash* by Trisha Henkes Noble
> *The Day Gogo Went to Vote* by Elaine Sisilu
> *The Relatives Came* by Cynthia Rylant
> *Snowflake Bentley* by Jacqueline Briggs Martin
> *Gooney Bird Greene* by Lois Lowry

As we read a picture book or student sample aloud, we can draw students' attention to the structural features of the genre. We might begin with a "Five W's" chart to show how the story orients the reader.

Title	Who	What	When	Where	Why

Later on, you'll want to return to some published memoirs to look at features of development and language.

Pre-writing

As students become familiar with the genre through reading, they will be ready to begin writing. For many young writers, whose experience in the world is limited, finding a topic is the hardest part of writing. A daily writing program, with many opportunities for self-selection of topics, is the best way to ensure that your students will be fluent and prolific writers. Nonetheless, it is worthwhile to spend some time modeling and guiding the students in generating ideas for writing. Two tools for gathering writing topics are the Personal Timeline and Writing Bingo, outlined in the mini-lessons below.

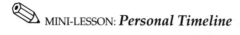

MINI-LESSON: *Personal Timeline*

Ask students to generate a graph of memorable events – good and not-so-good – in their lives. On a horizontal baseline, have them mark each of the years of their lives, then plot events on a scale of 1–10 (high points) or 1–10 (low points). (There should be roughly one event for each year of their lives.) This creative activity enables students to use artistic talents, as they can illustrate their memorable events with pictures or symbols. Often one of these events will become good material for a recount. An example appears below.

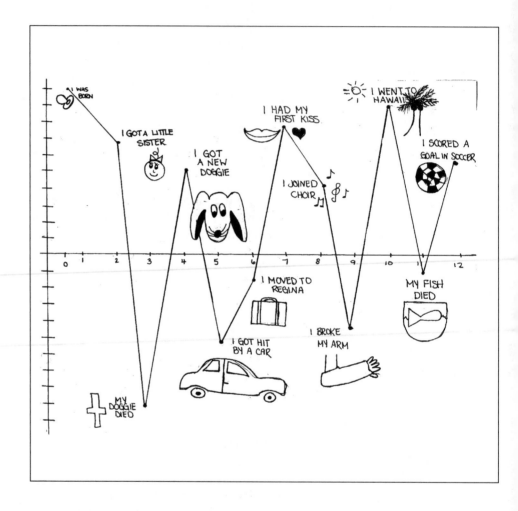

MINI-LESSON: *Writing Bingo*

Create a grid of sentence stems for students to complete (see page 63). The number of boxes will vary according to the maturity and needs of your students. (In fact, you may need to read the sentence stems aloud for some of them.) Make it a game by encouraging students to call "Bingo!" when they have "blacked out" the page by completing each square.

Here's an excerpt from a completed Writing Bingo chart:

My favorite holiday was	Something that once scared me was	I was really surprised when	At last
when we went to Calgary for the stampede.	*when I heard a noise in the basement and thought it was a ghost.*	*I got an 85 in math last year. I thought I was going to flunk.*	*I've got this grid finished so now I can go read a book. That's easier than writing.*

The Bingo game is another Lori favorite. She likes to leave one square blank, for students to write in an idea they got from someone else. See page 63 for a full version.

Again, the graphic organizer is simply a device to enable students to reflect on events in their own lives. It works well for several reasons:

- It seems like a game so students are more inclined to participate.
- Students may complete the squares in any order and leave out the ones they can't answer.
- The graphic organizer format is less intimidating to reluctant writers than a list or a blank piece of paper.

When you feel you have allocated enough time to filling the grid, ask each student to read aloud one of her squares. Doing this will provide time for other students to catch up and will also enable students to get ideas from one another. This activity is particularly important for those students whose lives don't provide a rich language or experiential background.

The completed Writing Bingo cards, Personal Timelines and any other idea-generating tools should be inserted into each student's writing portfolio as a reference for future writing. Now your students have a cache of ideas that may be turned into personal writing pieces.

A common problem for student writers is choosing topics that are too big. A memoir called "My Trip to Disneyland" is often a list of events or a much longer piece than any reader would want to read. It is far more effective to write a focused personal memoir called "My Wet Trip Down Splash Mountain."

Lori refers to the process of defining a topic's scope as "Skinnying Down the Topic" and includes it as a pre-writing task. Paul says that sometimes a writer has to overwrite about a topic and go back in to prune it during the revision stage. He calls this "Finding the Story." Whatever you call it, getting the topic down to a manageable size leads to a more effective, interesting piece of writing.

Making a plan

The "Topic Tree," found in Chapter 6, is a useful tool for refining memoir topics as well.

Once the topic is of reasonable size, the writer has to plan what he is going to say about it. Remind students that the purpose of a memoir is to entertain or inform readers by describing a series of events. Obviously, they will need to decide what those events will be.

Brainstorming is a starting point for generating ideas, but it doesn't help the writer organize those ideas into the logical sequence necessary for an effective recount. It may be necessary to take brainstorming a step further by numbering the events in the order that they will be described and eliminating those details that may not contribute to the main theme of the memoir. Another suggestion is to use colored markers to highlight the details that go together. For some students, writing each idea on a separate square of paper and physically sorting and grouping them works best.

✎ MINI-LESSON: *Teaching the Personal Memoir Organizer*

You may want to use the graphic organizer on page 64 to demonstrate how to plan a personal memoir. Start with the four squares in the centre, leaving the opening sentence and closing until later. Model each step of the way using your own topics and be sure to allow your students plenty of writing time to work on each section. If this lesson becomes unwieldy, it may be necessary to break it down into two or more mini-lessons.

Forms for a Personal Memoir

story
anecdote
diary
autobiography
newspaper article
poem
picture book

1. Have students select a "skinnied down" topic from one of their lists. Suggest that they choose something that they
   • have strong feelings about
   • can remember clearly
   • can describe vividly
   • would like to share with others
2. The top rectangle is for an opening sentence. Some writers find it easier to craft a lead after they have outlined the memoir; others like to start at the beginning. Remember that this organizer is just a record of initial thoughts. Because we want the students to get writing as quickly as possible, we will probably want to save a lesson on effective leads until later in the process. Students will then have an opportunity to revise and recraft their leads.
3. The four squares are designed to outline story ideas. The first box addresses the questions *who, what, when, where,* and *why*. Not all this information may be available or even necessary, but it creates a context for the recount. In each of the remaining three boxes, the writer notes one key event, essentially the beginning, middle and end of the story. The writer may use point form or even pictures. The purpose of the boxes is for the writer to generate and organize ideas, not to create finely crafted sentences.
4. The bottom rectangle is for a closing sentence. In a memoir, the closing sentence is often a statement of the writer's feelings about the experience or the lesson learned.

A sample personal memoir organizer is shown on the next page.

Personal Memoir Organizer

Topic: *Rafting on the pond with my cousin Julie*

Opening Sentence
My aunt warned us not to go rafting on the pond.

Who? *Julie and I* What? *Went rafting on the pond and the raft sank* When? *When we were 10* Where? *At Julie's farm* Why? *For adventure*	First *We snuck down to the pond* *- hiding from my aunt* *- behind the barn*
Next *rode on an old door* *- middle of pond, door sank* *- water not deep but cold* *- waded off in our jeans*	Finally *jeans soaking wet* *- took off our jeans and hung them in the treehouse* *- had to wait till they dried*

Closing

Did we learn a lesson shivering in the treehouse waiting for our jeans to dry?

For beginning writers, the information on the organizer will be enough to start developing a memoir. More advanced writers can be asked to add two or three details to each event, just as Lori did above. Each of the squares then becomes the structure of one or more paragraphs of text.

Remember that our goal is to provide our students with the tools they need to become independent learners. Once they have learned how to use the tools, they have to be able to use them in their own way.

Drafting

The organizer provides a skeleton which the writer uses to elaborate on rough ideas. With this structure in place, she is ready to pour ideas on paper in reasonably coherent form. Some will be in sentences and even paragraphs. There will be plenty of time for improving and correcting later.

In order to write the draft, the writer has certain decisions to make. What form should the writing take? Even within the personal memoir genre there are numerous alternatives: a diary entry, an autobiography, a news report. Should the memoir be told in the first-person or third? Is the writer part of the story or an outside observer? Who is likely to read this memoir? The nature of the audience will influence the tone and form of the writing.

Revising

In an effective writing program, students should have the opportunity to choose the pieces of writing that they want to revise and take to publication. This means that they need several rough drafts from which to choose. Maybe the tale of the ghost in the basement didn't develop very well or the sketch on the trip to Calgary came out too much like a list. Students should be able to pick writing that has potential before they begin revising.

When it comes to revision, every student's needs will be different. The following chart describes what an effective personal memoir looks like, using the Six Traits framework:

What an Effective Personal Memoir Looks Like

Ideas	Organization	Voice	Word Choice	Sentence Fluency	Conventions
Topic is focused; main theme is evident. There are strong supporting details – no gaps or extraneous information.	Ideas are clearly and logically organized. Transitions provide chronology. Lead hooks the reader's interest and the memoir wraps up neatly.	Writing reveals personality of the writer and arouses feeling in the reader. There is evidence that the writer cares about the topic.	Words are precise and carefully chosen to energize writing and create appropriate images and descriptions. Energetic verbs are used.	Writing is rhythmical and readable with good variety of sentence structure and length. Informal structures and dialogue may be used for effect.	Age- and risk-appropriate control of conventions – spelling, punctuation and grammar – makes the writing easy to read.

The first sentence of any piece of writing is like the door to an unfamiliar house. It can be inviting, or even enticing, or it can discourage the reader from entering. We want to teach students to open every piece of writing with a lead that hooks the reader's attention and pulls her in.

The mini-lesson below offers guidance on how to do that.

 MINI-LESSON: *Many Great Ways to Start a Piece of Writing*.

1. Have each student pull a novel or other book off the shelf and read the opening sentence. Discuss which sentences are effective "hooks" and why.

2. Put up the list "Six Great Ways to Start a Piece of Writing" (there's a poster on page 65). Have the students go on a treasure hunt for examples of each type of lead.

Here is a summary of the ways that students might begin their writing:

- with a question
- with dialogue
- with an interesting fact
- with a strong opinion or feeling
- with a single word or sentence fragment
- with something that leaves the reader wondering

Make a bulletin-board display and add to it on a regular basis.

3. Tell the students to choose any draft from their writing folders and examine the lead. Did they start too soon? (Openers such as "I got up this morning and ate my breakfast" don't really engage the reader.) Tell them to find the point at which the story actually begins and mark it.
4. Have students use one of the six techniques to develop a new lead.
5. For practice, you may want to have students write one of each of the six types of lead sentences and work with a partner to choose the one that suits their memoir best.

 MINI-LESSON: *Exploding a Moment*

A Grade 4 student named James wrote this memoir.

> *Last week we went to my Grandma's in Calgary. I got up in the morning and put on my Calgary Flames sweatshirt. I ate a bowl of Cheerios for breakfast. Then I packed my suitcase with my pyjamas, my toothbrush, some clean clothes and a few toys. We all piled in the car. On the way, my dad hit a patch of ice and slid into a tree. When we got to my Grandma's we had sausage and perogies for supper. I got to sleep on the floor in a sleeping bag. It was fun.*

The problem is one of balance. What James ate for supper gets as much attention as the car crashing into a tree!

Sometimes we have to teach students to slow down and focus on the key ideas. Barry Lane calls this "exploding a moment." What if James were to take the exact moment when the car started to skid out of control and tell it in slow motion? He could take that 60-second time frame and break it down into three or four or five or six sentences. Not only would it provide some interest and suspense, it would signal to the reader that this incident is the most interesting and exciting part of the story.

Put James's story on an overhead and read it with the students. Ask them to find a place where they could explode the moment. Together, re-create that event in four or five sentences, for example:

Dad slammed on the brakes, but the car kept going.

Slowly it slid sideways across the highway.

Thunk! The front of the car slid into an old maple tree.

Dad took off his seatbelt and leaped out of the car to check the damage.

He groaned when he saw a large V-shaped dent in the bumper.

Tell the students to find a place in their own draft writing that they could explode a moment. They may want to signal this point with a revision symbol such as ☆

Exploding a moment is a great strategy for adding detail to the main theme of the story. It links well with Paul's "Finding the Story" strategy. Generally, the moment to explode is the real story in the rough draft.

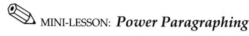 MINI-LESSON: *Power Paragraphing*

The basic means of organizing a memoir, as well as most other types of writing, is the paragraph. Generally speaking, a paragraph is a group of sentences that develop one topic or idea. For young students, we try to develop longer and more articulated paragraphs. For older students, we want to show the effectiveness of a very short paragraph in dialogue or for exclamation.

Use "Power Paragraphing" on page 66 to introduce students to guidelines on when to start a new paragraph. Look at "Blood Bath" on page 61 and talk about why each paragraph begins where it does. Then look at a story such as "The Game" on page 59 and have students work in pairs to rework the piece into paragraphs. (Note: Different groups will have different paragraph structures – and that's just fine as long as they can justify their choices.)

MINI-LESSON: *Cutting the Clutter*

One of the main problems in memoir writing is including too much information. Some young writers want to tell us every detail from the moment they woke up in the morning till the time they went to bed – virtually a "toothbrush to toothbrush" story!

In memoir writing, as in all good writing, the writer must decide *where* the story is. The details he includes should clarify and support the main idea, not distract from it.

Cutting out material is the hardest part of revising. It's often quite hard for a novice writer to distance himself from the writing enough to decide what doesn't need to be there. After all, he has labored over every word. And somewhere along the line he has gotten the impression that longer is better. How can making a story shorter make it better?

Practising with someone else's piece of writing is a good way to help students pay attention to what's important in a story and what can be deleted. Go back and read the story that James wrote about his trip to Grandma's. Which details do little to move the story along? Talk about the memoir as a group and cross out the sentences that seem to offer extraneous detail.

Then have students revisit one of their own drafts to find information that isn't important to the story. Since they will likely find it hard to delete information from their own writing, you may want to have students work with partners to help them "weed" their "gardens."

Editing and Publishing

By now your students should have several rough drafts in their writing folders. They've worked on one or two to revise and apply the mini-lessons on leads, exploding a moment, paragraphing and cutting the clutter.

Before they publish a piece of writing, it's important to make sure all the *i*'s are dotted and the *t*'s are crossed. A story should be error-free before it is published.

Choose your editing mini-lessons from the kinds of errors your students are making in their writing. There is no point in teaching question marks if all of your students are using them correctly. There is no point in teaching quotation marks if your students aren't ready for dialogue in their writing.

Being able to proofread their own work is an essential skill for students – and adults, too. Have your kids practise on someone else's work first. Use the tips in Chapter 1. Then resign yourself to being your students' final editor before they publish.

 MINI-LESSON: *Title Tales*

Paul's working title for his first teen novel was "Danny's book." When he sent it to publishers in 1976, he called the manuscript *Only Wilts Wear Glasses*. Putnam thought that might offend readers who wore glasses, so it was published as *Wilted* in 1978, and later reprinted as *You've Seen Enough*.

A good title gives a hint about what the memoir or story is about, without giving away too much. It should be fairly short – preferably no more than five words – and it should entice the reader to read on.

Have your students choose a favorite published book or story and come up with three alternative titles. Model the process by brainstorming other titles for a familiar book. For example, *Charlotte's Web* might also be called *Saving Wilbur*, "*Some Pig*" or even *A Barnyard Tale*.

Then have your students choose one of their drafts, create at least three titles and survey their friends about which one is most effective.

Remind them that the first word in a title, and all other key words, should be capitalized. "Glue words," like *from, to, for* or *the*, do not need capitals unless they are the first or last word in the title.

Sharing the work

How can students share a personal memoir with an audience? Some suggestions for publishing include these:

- Rewrite or word-process the memoir neatly on paper.
- Display some on a bulletin board with the caption "Days of Our Lives."
- Add illustrations or graphics.

Remember

Students don't always want their personal recounts shared. It's important to discuss the difference between personal writing and published writing.

- Make a photo-journal or PowerPoint presentation showing pictures of the event.
- Read the memoir out loud to someone, perhaps the principal or an adult volunteer.
- Make the memoir into a book.
- Give the memoir as a gift to parents or someone else who can relate to the story.

The personal memoir is a great way to start the year's writing program or to introduce the writing process, regardless of the student age. It honors students' experiences and gives them a foundation from which to build both writing skills and craft.

What's for Dinner?
by Brennan, Grade 3

One Thanksgiving, our family went to my Uncle Nick's farm. My dog Midas and I wanted to help Uncle Nick catch a turkey. We went into the muddy pen. Midas chased the turkey. He bonked his head and fell into the trough. My shoe got stuck in the mud and I fell face forward. We had steak for supper instead of turkey!

My Dirt Bike
by Alicia, Grade 4

One day I was out on my dirt bike. When I came into my yard I slipped in some sand. I burned my leg. I didn't cry until I was upstairs telling my Mom what happened. We were going to the lake that day, so Mom put cold water on my leg. It stung a lot and I was screaming my head off! My Mom and Dad put a bandage on the burn. Suddenly my Dad said to my mom that we should go see a doctor.

My Dad went over the speed limit to get me to the doctor. When I saw the doctor, he put me on the bed with curtains around it. The doctor gave my mom lots of stuff for my leg.

It was not a nice week-end! I couldn't go tubing or water skiing. I did not like it at all!

When I got back from the lake my Dad fixed the dirt bike, but I couldn't ride for a long time.

The Game
by Tyler, Grade 5

There were five minutes left in the game at Edmonton Sky Reach Centre. The score was tied two to two. Suddenly, Finland got a clear cut breakaway from centre ice. The winger came at me like a jet. I backed in with him like two lions who had spotted a scrap of meat a mile away and were racing to get it. Sweat was running down my face like a fountain. He wound up for a slapshot. I was in position. I was ready. Smack! His stick hit the puck. The puck came at me like a bullet, landing in my glove, almost breaking the webbing. There was a face-off to the left of me. It was ended with a blocker save and another cover. The next face-off was to the right. This time my team got the puck. They were skating and passing up the ice like the wind. Suddenly Gonie, our star player, found an opening. What a wrist shot! He and the goalie had a scuffle for the puck. Gonie took the puck and passed it back to Currie. He wound up and took a slapshot. He scored. Our team had won the Junior League Tournament.

A Trip to Mars
by Carly, Grade 6

Well, of course it's true! It did go exactly like this, Mrs. Trefiak! No lie!

The moon, our usual vacation spot, was completely booked up. Even the campgrounds were packed. The word must have gotten out that the hot springs in the craters are awesome. So, of course, Mars was the logical alternative. It's close, and the cost of rocketship tickets and accommodations are way less than Saturn. Plus, it's red!

We had to get up early to catch the morning rocket. West Rocket may be cheap, but it flies way too early in the morning. Let me tell you, though, the freeze-dried pretzels were absolutely delicious.

We stopped at the moon for lunch: green cheese sandwiches. Whoever said that the moon isn't made of green cheese was completely WRONG. That is the best cheese I've ever had. Of course, it turned my teeth green.

Green aliens from Pluto with huge heads and three fingers hijacked us when we were halfway to Mars. They turned the ship around to Jupiter and we were about to crash into one of its moons when Marvin the Martian and his dog saved us, and . . .
What?! D minus and a note to see the school counselor???????!!!

The Meaning of Freedom to My Family
by Phuong, Grade 7

I will tell you about my parents' escape from Vietnam. It starts off when my dad was 24 and my mom was 20.

In 1975, Vietnam was under Communist government. Both of my grandpas worked with the democratic government, so when the Communist government took over, both of my families could not have any freedom. They weren't allowed to express their feelings, they weren't allowed to find a job, and they couldn't go to University.

They looked outside the world to find a place that had freedom. It took several years to plan their escape . . .

It was 1981 when my parents came to Canada. My parents did not even have one cent. The Canadian government helped them out to find an apartment and to put them in school to learn English. By that time my mom was pregnant with my brother. And from then on my parents worked hard and became successful in business. My parents each own a business now.

Everything turned out well in the end. Freedom meant everything to the people on the boat and that is why my mom lost her cousin. We'd always pray that wherever she is now, God will watch over her.

And that is how much freedom meant to my family.

Student Writing

Blood Bath

by Todd, Grade 7

"B-a-a-a-ck!" the chicken squawked helplessly. Flapping wildly in my hand, it struggled helplessly as it bled to death. Its warm blood splattered my face.

"Hey, rookie! It's chicken time!" Glen yelled. I glanced at my watch – 7:10 a.m. – and I sat up and struggled into my work clothes.

When I walked in, Glen was already sharpening the knives. "Go fetch some chickens from the barn and make sure they're the big ones."

As the barn loomed in front of me, my stomach knotted. I trudged slowly towards it. As soon as I entered the warm building, the smell of chicken dung stung my nostrils. It was nearly as disgusting as what was to come.

Mike and David snatched three chickens and handed me two. Their soft yellow felt smelled horrible. The stench was like spoiled milk with a hint of compost. The odour reminded me of the smell of vomit.

Carrying two chickens, I hurried toward the chopping block. Glen was waiting with the axe in his hand. I gave him a chicken. It weighed about six pounds. "Whoa! Good one!" he exclaimed as he placed the chicken's head between two rusty nails which were hammered into a sawhorse. The chicken stared blankly into Glen's eyes. It had no way of knowing what was coming. Glen tightened his grip on the axe, wound up and . . .

"Smack!" The chicken's head rolled to the ground. Blood was flying everywhere. Glen and I traded chickens. I clenched the dead chicken with my blood-stained hands. Glen looked at me and smirked, "Can you handle it?"

I smiled weakly. "Oh, yeah," I lied. A wave of nausea swept over me. Glen handed me the other decapitated chicken. To myself I thought, "Die, chickens! Die!'"

The headless chickens were now flapping so wildly that I felt like I was going to be lifted off the ground. I closed my eyes and waited for the feathered monsters' nerves to die.

Later that evening I was back home and watching television. The thoughts of butchering chickens were still rolling through my head and my stomach was still a bit queasy. As I sat down to eat my peanut butter sandwich, the phone rang.

"Hello?" I answered.

"Hey, Todd," Glen's voice echoed through the speaker. "You busy tomorrow?"

The End of the Line
by Alex, Grade 8

The nervous waves continually washed over him. The drawing that he was working on was looking spectacular, but with every stroke, every push, the carefully placed lines would begin to widen. Thicker and thicker they grew, until finally, he knew that the time had come.

This gut-wrenching moment had been happening for innumerable generations in his family. His father, his grandfather, even his grandfather's grandfather had all experienced this cherished moment in their lives. He even knew what it would feel like, for the memory had been embedded in his family's instincts. It was something that was unavoidable, and fate had bounced him along through life, but the whole time doom had been waiting for him. It need not wait any longer, for he was ready.

He held back the tears as he ceased to draw for the last time.

He was driven in, twisted, and shoved into the strange machine he knew all too well. But this time, he heard the sound of metal clashing metal. That was the sign. It was the moment his whole species had to, and would eventually, confront.

The pencil's last sharpening.

We might debate the genre of this piece – but it's great writing, regardless.

Writing Bingo

My favorite holiday was	Something that once scared me was	I was really surprised when	At last
I felt ripped off when	I got this scar from	A really dumb thing I did was	I like it when my family
When I was little	Someone did a nice thing for me when	I was so mad when	I couldn't believe that
I'll never forget the time when	I got blamed for something I didn't do when	I was never so happy to see anyone as	I laughed so hard when

Personal Memoir Organizer

Topic: _____

Opening Sentence

Who?	First
What?	
When?	
Where?	
Why?	
Next	Finally

Closing

Six Great Ways to Start a Piece of Writing

1. With a question

What could be scarier than spending a night in a haunted house?

2. With dialogue

"I dare you to stay in there past midnight," my brother said.

3. With an interesting fact

According to surveys, half of all adults believe in the supernatural and one person in ten claims to have seen a ghost.

4. With a strong opinion or feeling

There's no such thing as ghosts!

5. With a single word or sentence fragment

Me? Scared?

6. With something that leaves the reader wondering

There was a sound in the basement, and I knew it wasn't just a mouse.

Power Paragraphing

Zap up your writing with power paragraphs. Paragraphs not only make sense of your ideas, they can add vim, vigor and voltage to what you write.

Start a new paragraph when

- a new person speaks
- the story has moved to a new place
- you're bringing in a new idea
- you're introducing a different point of view

Always use a paragraph when

- you're introducing a theme or story
- you're building an argument step by step
- you've reached your conclusion

You might want to use a very short paragraph

- for punch
- for surprise
- for humor

You might want to forget about paragraphs when . . . you want to bore your readers to death!

5

Our Plot Thickens – The Fictional Narrative

Of all the literary genres, the fictional narrative – the short story – is the most familiar to young readers. We read stories to children long before they begin school and continue long after they can read to themselves. We talk about many of the elements of a story as early as Kindergarten. We ask kids to write and illustrate stories as soon as they can hold a pencil.

Although fictional narrative writing may seem easy, it is the most difficult genre to do well. Just ask Paul, who makes his living writing novels! Fiction is the only genre that requires the writer to generate ideas completely out of his own imagination. In writing a personal memoir, the writer retells an event or series of events that have happened to him or her. In most expository and persuasive writing, the writer is able to rely on research and other sources for information. But the fictional narrative requires the writer to create characters, build a story, and then put it all together in a convincing way.

For this reason, we suggest that you lay the groundwork for Writing Workshop and work on the personal memoir before tackling the realm of fiction. In this chapter, we offer a step-by-step guide to helping your students write fictional narratives, from creating characters to developing plot, conflict and resolution. There is a great deal of material here, so be sure to choose the topics and mini-lessons based on your students' specific needs.

The Difference Between Fictional Narrative and Memoir

Ironically, a fictional narrative *can* be based on a true situation and a memoir *can* be based on a fictional event. One major difference is in the structure of the story. A memoir is often episodic; it is based on a central idea revealed through a series of events. A short story is essentially a problem that must be solved by a character or characters. It is the unfolding of events that becomes important in the story, building to a wonderful conclusion.

It's amazing how many short stories and novels can be summarized in four easy pieces:

Somebody *(Character)*
Wanted *(Goal)*
But *(Conflict or Problem)*
So *(Resolution)*

Here are a few examples from literature that will be familiar to most of you:

Mr. Arable wanted to slaughter Wilbur the pig, but Charlotte spun words into her web to make everyone think that Wilbur was special, so Wilbur's life was saved.

Voldemort, the Dark Lord, wanted the Philosopher's Stone so he could come back to power, but Harry Potter and his friends didn't want evil to rise again so they thwarted him and the stone was destroyed.

Miss Nelson wanted her students to behave, but they were rude and unruly, so she disguised herself as a mean substitute teacher named Miss Viola Swamp.

Below is a summary of the characteristics of fictional narrative:

FICTIONAL NARRATIVE FRAMEWORK

Purpose	**Organization**
To entertain, to tell a story, to teach a lesson	BEGINNING: Grabs the reader with interesting characters in a situation or problem that must be resolved MIDDLE: Adds additional complications to the plot END: Wraps up the story line(s) and sometimes makes a general statement about the human condition or offers a moral
	Language Features
	✽ Uses different levels of language formality depending on narrative voice ✽ May be told in first- or third-person voice ✽ Generally told in the past tense ✽ Features dialogue for up to one-half of the story ✽ Often makes use of description, symbolism and figurative language
	Examples
	Short story, novel, novella, fairy tale, tall tale, parable, fable

Reading as Writers

Your students have had plenty of experience with reading and listening to fictional narratives. Now they must learn to *read as writers*. Normally, readers read a story to be entertained, to get lost in another time and place, to explore new worlds. Writers read a story to get ideas.

"A writer is always scrounging ideas and techniques from other writers," Paul says. "That's how we learn." So any fiction writing unit must begin by reading plenty of well-written stories and paying close attention to the writer's craft: how he engages the reader in the story, how he develops characters, how he builds suspense, and how he keeps the reader wondering about the story's outcome.

Choose an appropriate short story to read aloud. Read the story once to get the meaning, then read it again to look at the writer's craft. It's always fun to present scary stories before Halloween, so you might do a reading of Edgar Allan Poe's "The Pit and the Pendulum." Some questions to consider on second reading might be these: Does the opening hook our interest? ("I was sick — sick unto death with that long agony . . . ") Why did the author start a new paragraph here, or there? Does the dialogue give us insight into the character or situation? How does the author build up the tension? Is the ending satisfactory or contrived? This kind of discussion lays the groundwork for your students' own writing.

Picture books are wonderful resources for showing students of any age how to develop characters and plots. They're short, usually straightforward in their characterization and plot development, and contain wonderful language and ideas to engage even sophisticated middle-schoolers. Here are some good titles:

The Very First, Last Time by Jan Andrews
Fanny's Dream by Carolyn Buehner
Saving Sweetness by Diane Stanley
Herschel and the Hannukah Goblins by Eric Kimmel
The True Story of the Three Little Pigs by Jon Scieszka

Just as we created a "Five W's" chart (see page 49) for reading personal narrative writing, it will be useful to create an "SWBS" chart for noting fictional narrative structure:

Somebody	Wanted	But	So

As well as looking at overall story structure, remind students to pay particular attention to the way authors develop their characters. Usually we learn about a character from what he says, what he does, what he thinks, what others say about him and what the author says about him. A thoughtful reading of picture books will offer examples.

Only six plot structures are the basis of virtually all fictional writing, from Shakespeare to Dr. Seuss. Here they are:

- character with problem or goal
- character versus nature
- good guys versus bad guys
- boy meets girl
- lost is found
- mystery gets solved

What Drives a Story?

Many people think that narrative fiction is plot-driven, but many people are frequently wrong. Stories are not driven by the plot; the plot is driven by the characters. Unless the reader cares about what happens to the characters, the story can't go forward, or it does so without effect. Who cares about keeping the Philosopher's Stone away from Lord Voldemort unless we care about Harry Potter? Who cares about catching Moriarty unless we care about Sherlock Holmes? Plot is important, but character is the key.

This concept may be the hardest idea for students in school to grasp. Lots of students, especially boys, like to create stories just like those they see on TV, but without the visuals and weekly buildup that television provides. The result is an underdeveloped, uninteresting catalogue of astonishing events often leading to the deaths of hundreds of minor characters due to car crashes, machine guns or outer-space altercations. Creating such stories may be great fun for the writer, but reading them will be tedious for the rest of us.

So we have to show our students that character is the heart of the story. In good fictional narrative, the character has a problem to solve or a goal to achieve. External problems and internal flaws are the elements that create suspense and interest in a story. These conflicts are often typified as character against character, character against society, character against the environment, or even character against self.

The plot follows from all this.

✎ MINI-LESSON: *Somebody . . . Wanted . . . But . . . So . . .*

The Mysteries of Harris Burdick by Chris Van Allsburg is a wonderful collection of mysterious pictures that can be used as springboards for generating story ideas starting with "SWBS."

Earlier, we suggested that you begin by summarizing familiar stories using this "SWBS" format. Now have your students work in pairs to make up plot summaries for their own stories.

Demonstrate using the following sentence stem:

The kids wanted to _____ .

But _____

So _____ .

Then generate some other "SWBS" exercises for practice:

• The tired teacher wanted . . .
• The famous athlete wanted . . .
• The anxious father wanted . . .

Keep this exercise short – you're just developing ideas for stories. Writing the stories themselves will come later.

All too often, students want to include the name of everyone in their class – and especially their friends – in the story. This makes for a confusing muddle. Best to limit a short story to one main character and no more than two or three secondary characters.

Pre-writing

There is a popular assumption (perpetuated by second-rate Hollywood films) that writers simply start to write and the story comes to them as if by magic. In truth, there is little serendipity in writing. Most writers create an explicit plan for their stories before beginning.

Although the story may take different turns once begun, or during revision, a good writer leaves little to chance. Paul always develops an outline before he begins a novel. "That gives me the freedom to change without the danger of getting lost." Dickens covered walls with the notes for his novels and their dozens of characters; Dostoevsky filled notebooks, sometimes describing a single character for 60 pages. The point is simple: professional writers don't just start writing – they plan the story ahead of time.

This planning is even more important for novice writers. When students take time to plot their story (pun intended) before drafting, their writing is likely to be tighter, more focused and more effectively crafted.

The pre-writing plan should include these components:

- a well-developed character
- the character's goal or problem
- one or more problems, complications or challenges
- some form of resolution

Aspects of character and plot are explored in the following pages.

Character

A good plan begins with a well-developed character. Too many students think a character description involves only what a character looks like. Real character is far more than that: personality, background (or "backstory," as the screenwriters say), values, and relationships. The writer should know her character intimately in order to make credible judgments about how that character will respond to the struggles he confronts. Although a writer may not use all the information she develops about the character, a thorough description of his appearance, personality, motivations and tastes is a good starting point for the narrative.

Paul prefers to get models for his characters from real life – former students, people he has met, even his own kids – then add fictional traits and experiences. Other writers create copious notes about each character. Mystery writer Eric Wilson cuts magazine pictures of his characters to help him picture them as he writes. All of these techniques give a character "face." What's needed next is personality.

The foundation for creating a personality will be the problem that the character must overcome or the goal she wants to achieve. What does the character hope to accomplish by the end of the book? Or what do you, as a writer, hope for her to accomplish, even though she may not be aware of it at the outset? How will her life or her world or the people around her be different as a result of her actions? What obstacles or conflicts will stand in her way? Will there be setbacks? Will she succeed?

Visualization

It has been said that you can't write what you can't see. Sometimes having students draw a character helps them get a clearer picture of the character's appearance and personality.

Literary characters can be either minor figures whom we see only in passing or fully developed characters who drive a story; in other words, they can be *flat* or *fat*. Flat characters have little personality; as readers we don't know them very well and don't have a lot of interest in what happens to them. Fat characters are well-rounded. We know about their habits, their tastes, their strengths and their flaws.

A writer should know more about his characters than may be revealed in the story. This knowledge is how he determines what problems the character will experience, how the character will respond to things that happen to her and how the problem will be resolved. Often a character will reveal more of herself to the author as a story proceeds, but it's always easier if a writer thinks first and writes later.

There are a number of exercises we can undertake to help our students do that thinking.

 MINI-LESSON: *Character Brainstorm*

We all write best when we can start with what we know. Instead of using imaginary characters such as mermaids, aliens and dragons, why not make a list of the kinds of people we might encounter in our lives? Give the students a few examples, then invite their suggestions to fill this bingo grid.

The playground bully	A principal with a great sense of humor	A painfully shy girl	A computer genius
A boy who loves hockey	A dancer with a broken leg		

MINI-LESSON: *Character Fastwrite*

The fastwrite is a technique that can be used for many purposes. A stopwatch and a time limit can have an amazing effect on even the most reluctant writer. In this case, we want to generate a quick character profile. Give students this prompt:

_____ is a _____ who . . .

For example: *Mr. Witherspoon is a jolly principal who loves to make his students laugh. He is constantly playing practical jokes.*

Time the students for three minutes. At the end of the time, call stop and have them count the number of words they wrote. Share a few of the results, including your own. We sometimes find that our students are better at this (or any of these exercises) than we are.

Repeat the exercise, having the students choose another character. They inevitably write more words the second time.

If your students are responding well to this exercise, you may even want to repeat it a third time. At this point, your students will have introduced themselves to three characters that could appear in future writing.

MINI-LESSON: *Character Interview*

Have your students choose one of their three characters from "Character Fastwrite" – or come up with a new character – to "fatten up." Together, develop a list of interview questions that they should answer about the character. Here are some starters:

1. What is your greatest strength?
2. What is one of your weaknesses?
3. What things do you like to do?
4. What things really bug you?
5. What is one of the highlights of your life?
6. What is one of the saddest moments of your life?

Students then choose several questions and make jot-note responses from one character's perspective.

Plot development: Goal, conflict and resolution

Paul: I always insist on an outline before the students can begin their drafts. As a working writer, I need to produce an outline before I get a contract. Why shouldn't the kids?

Lori: I find that when students try to write without a plan, their stories tend to be rambling and disjointed – the classic case of bang-up beginnings, mediocre middles and crummy conclusions.

Once a writer gets to know a character, he will have a better sense of what kinds of problems the character might experience. For example, a sarcastic practical joker might turn all his friends against him. A video game addict might lose track of time and miss an important appointment. In addition to basics such as appearance and personality, an important aspect of a character's development is the goal she is trying to achieve and the problems she needs to overcome en route to that goal. Whether it's retrieving the Holy Grail, winning a hockey game or finding popularity in a new school, a central character *should always have a goal.* When this goal is established as part of the characterization, it enables the writer to flesh out the story more effectively.

But what makes a story "work" are the problems and conflicts that the character encounters as she strives to achieve her goal. These events keep the reader engaged and wanting to read on. Just when the central character seems about to achieve the goal, some new problem makes that goal seem still further out of reach. The result – the reader wants to keep on reading.

At the end of the story, of course, the reader needs a resolution. Again, knowing the character enables the writer to come up with a credible solution to the character's problem. All too often, student writers resort to cop-outs such as "It was all a dream" or "Vlastomorf was dead . . . or was he?" that simply let the reader down.

While it is possible – and sometimes even desirable – to maintain a *little* flexibility about the ending, it always helps to start a story with some ending in mind. Will the character achieve her goal? Will she find herself moving in a different direction than when she began? Will she change in any way from the beginning of the story to the end? Maybe she will decide that her original goal wasn't what she really wanted after all.

Starting with the end in mind will enable the writer to choose obstacles and reactions that move the story forward in a meaningful and focused way.

Before they begin to draft the actual story, have the students select one of the characters they have developed and brainstorm possible goals, conflicts and resolutions. (See "Plot Brainstorm" on page 88.) From these alternatives they will be able to select a plot line to further develop.

 MINI-LESSON: *Tell the Story Out Loud*

Telling a story aloud is an important precursor to writing for the youngest writers and is useful for more mature writers as well. It enables them to formulate their ideas before writing and removes one layer of "working memory" when the writer begins to draft. It also enables the writer to organize her thoughts and work out some of the gaps and inconsistencies in her story plan.

Put the students in pairs and give each student two minutes to tell his story to his partner. There is no need for feedback. After exactly two minutes, announce, "Switch!" and the other partner tells his story. Repeat the exercise with new pairs, then repeat it a third time. By now, the students have had a chance to hear themselves tell their own stories and to make mental revisions and improvements.

Drafting

Rules for Drafting

1. Leave a space between lines.
2. Write on only one side of the paper.
3. Write in pen.
4. Don't erase – just cross out and keep on going.
5. Spell as well as you can – you can fix up your work later on.

Careful and detailed planning should make writing the first draft a much easier task than writing it without. Unfortunately, many writers experience the terrible panic that can set in when confronted with a blank computer screen or an empty sheet of paper.

Here's Paul's trick: Write *something*. Fill the empty space. Write down the title. Write a first sentence. If the student freezes up, give her the first sentence. (The first sentence is often thrown away later on, regard-less.) If the second sentence won't come, write the first sentence over.

And so it goes. Once the writing begins to flow – as long as that takes – it often keeps flowing. Paul always advises students not to look back. "Don't fix up your first sentence until you've written your last sentence or you'll never get done." Spelling, grammar, logic, development . . . none of that is critical right now. Just write.

✎ MINI-LESSON: *Writing in the Round*

To teach kids how to write fast and furiously, try this exercise. Arrange your students in something like a circle. Tell the kids they are going to write a three-part story. The central character of the story is the person to their immediate left. The story can be anything (but suitable for family entertainment since you'll read them aloud later) and the first writer won't have to finish it, just start it. Give them three minutes.

After exactly three minutes, call out: "Time's up. Move your papers to the right – away from the person you were just writing about." All the papers move; curiosity grows.

Then explain: "Your job is to write the middle of the story in front of you. Not *your* story, the story that's in front of you. You have a minute to read it and two minutes to add a few sentences. Go!"

After three minutes, the papers again move to the right. Your instruction is obvious: "You have one minute to read and three minutes to *finish* the story in front of you. This may seem impossible, but do the best you can."

And then watch the students write. Often they will beg for a little more time on this last section, and that's fine. Then share the results. The kids will laugh because they are the central characters, and they'll be amazed that they've written 150 or 200 or 300 words in just ten minutes.

There should always be a *next* story. Often the first story is just a warm-up for another story that the student wants to tell. When students see how exciting and successful they are with guidance, they will surely be motivated to write more. That's one more reason to expect students to draft at least three stories in this unit, though only one may make it all the way to publication.

While teaching kids how to draft and revise, Paul likes to begin each session with a warm-up exercise. These little practice pieces, like "Writing in the Round," develop only a paragraph or two. Sometimes the sparks from these exercises will lead to more elaborated writing later on; sometimes not. In any event, writing exercises get the pen moving on paper, just as a warm-up before a game gets the blood flowing through the veins.

Boys, barf and bloodshed

More and more teachers in middle-school classrooms are becoming aware that there's a "boy problem" in both reading and writing. Statistically, boys don't read as much as girls; they don't comprehend what they read as well as girls; and their test scores decline every year. Similarly, boys tend to write with less sophistication, use a more limited vocabulary and write less than girls. In the United States, the NAEP testing shows that the gap between boy and girl writing gets greater with each grade. In Canada, provincial testing shows that achievement gap begins in Grade 3.

Regardless, our job in the classroom is to bring *all* our students, both boys and girls, to a higher level. In writing, that means we have to focus some additional energy on encouraging greater sophistication, longer length, and greater subtlety ("You attacked aliens in your last story. What other ideas can you think of?").

One problem is that many boys want to replicate in print what they watch on television. They end up creating stories that have the action of cartoons and space sagas, but lack the sophistication in character and plot that we expect in written work. For boys, it can be a badge of honor to be killed off in a piece of writing created by their best friend. As teachers, we have to recognize this truth. Conversely, we can encourage writers to keep their buddies alive and to remember that their writing should be suitable for a public audience.

Some teachers and school districts forbid any violence in story-writing. All this does, however, is suppress the offending writing and drive it underground, where it bubbles right into high school. Other teachers feel that it's okay to let students write anything they want, however repetitive or repugnant it may be.

We favor a middle ground. There is no sense invalidating the interests of half the kids in your classroom – whether it's barf and bloodshed or Barbies and babysitters – when these can be useful motivators for good writing. But writing that goes to publication has an obligation not just to the writer, but to the readers. Overly violent and offensive works have no place in a school environment. Paul's rule is simple: "You can write what you want, but anything you read out loud or post in this classroom cannot offend my mother if she comes to visit." That Paul's mother never came to visit was irrelevant; her persona represented a standard of decorum. It's far easier to say, "My mother wouldn't tolerate this," than to go into lengthy arguments with students about the propriety of gruesome killings in print. In his parenting book *I'll Be the Parent, You Be the Kid*, Paul maintains that kids want and need limits, even when they rail against them. Maintain reasonable limits on violence and gore, and your students are likely to outgrow it.

And encourage the boys to move on to other topics and genres. It saddens us to see so many gifted middle-schoolers stuck in a world of fantasy writing with one-dimensional characters and little emotional or thematic development. If there are to be three finished pieces at the end of this unit, surely one action-adventure saga is enough. Introducing students to the genres and writing activities in this book will extend their skills – and, we hope, their interests.

Exploring the Elements of Fiction

The short story is a difficult genre. To write a piece successfully, students have to be familiar with many elements that bedevil even adult writers: leads, conclusions, dialogue and point of view. There is no ideal sequence for teaching these items. Rather, we suggest that you analyze your students' writing and pick the topics that most need work.

Write a strong lead

The opening of the fictional narrative serves two purposes: to hook the reader's attention and to set the stage for the story by introducing the characters, the setting and the problem.

Many students have trouble crafting an engaging lead. All too often, young writers open their writing with "One day," "Once upon a time," – or variations thereof. Teach students that this type of introduction works only for a certain type of story and sets the reader up to expect a tale of long ago and far away. One tedious form is the "breakfast to bed" story, which might start with "Hi, my name is Jeff" and continue with minutiae of Jeff's day, most of which have little to do with the story's main issue. Again, reading both good and bad examples of written work is the best cure for these writing maladies.

Make a display of effective leads from books and stories. It can be fun and effective to generate a chart featuring "Really Great Leads" and "Really Bad Leads" (which students can invent). Revisit "Six Great Ways to Start a Piece of Writing" from Chapter 4. For their own stories, have the kids try different kinds of leads. It is a good exercise to write at least two leads for any story and then choose the most effective. Professional writers usually go through a dozen.

Start in the middle

A good question for student writers is, *How close to the main event can I start?* Strange as it may sound, stories should not necessarily begin at the beginning. Many young writers spend so much time setting up the story that they run out of steam before they come to the main event.

One piece of good advice for young writers is to start in the middle of the action. Aristotle advised writers to start *in medias res* – in the middle of things – more than 2000 years ago and that advice still stands. Writers can always flash back to supporting events, but a story must focus on the key problem or challenge right away. Paul frequently advises his adult students to throw away their first page – or even their first chapter – if they want a more effective start. Your younger students can often sacrifice a paragraph without loss and sometimes with considerable gain.

Create some dialogue

Dialogue is a key element in fictional narrative, often making up as much as half of the story. Students usually need a review of the conventions – quotation marks, punctuation, and paragraphing when a new person speaks. But what they most need is an awareness of how to shape dialogue.

Too much student writing is peppered with the kind of dialogue the kids share on the phone or on Internet chats:

"Hi."

"Hi."

"What are you doing?"

"Nothing. What are you doing?"

"Nothing. You want to do something?"

"Sure. What do you want to do?"

Whoever first advised writers to "write as you talk" never heard typical kid conversations. The reality is that oral language conventions include a degree of repetition, ambiguity and monotony that written text will not tolerate.

The purpose of dialogue is to serve as a tool for defining character. Remember that two of the ways readers learn about a character is by what he says and what others say about him. Rarely does dialogue move the action along. (When was the last time you read a line like, "Do you want to go attack the aliens from outer space who have just landed outside room 8 and are threatening Mrs. Jones?") Action needs action, not talk, but characters need effective dialogue.

Students often have trouble with shifting tenses as they write. Most stories are written in the past tense, by convention. Some first-person stories can be told in the present tense for a kind of breathless effect, but this can get tedious over long stretches. Most kids are better off starting and staying in the past tense.

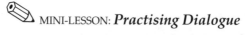

 MINI-LESSON: *Practising Dialogue*

Paul practises dialogue with students by having two students act out a scenario. "Haley, you're sitting in the cafeteria eating a hamburger when Jonah comes up to ask you to the Halloween Hop." "Andrew, you left Corey's bike behind your dad's truck and he ran over it." When your students improvise a scene, write down everything they say on an overhead transparency or computer screen.

The dialogue that your student actors make up will probably be terrible. But then give students a chance to work with the transcribed text. They can refine, embellish or change the dialogue altogether. The finished mini-stories are invariably great fun to read aloud.

Sharing a character's internal dialogue is another device that writers can use. It can be an effective way to create suspense or give a character more depth. Have students look for a place in their stories where they can add a character's question or self-doubt, for example: *Would he ever have a chance to see Wayne Gretzky in person? What will I tell my mother?*

Decide on a point of view

Almost all fairy tales are written from a third-person point of view. Most young-adult novels are written from a first-person point of view. Mystery stories are usually third-person; personal memoirs are almost always first-person. What works best? Try each to find out.

Every story has a point of view or narrative voice with which it is told. The two most common are third-person (a global view of the entire action) and first-person (a story seen and told by one character). The third-person point of view is the traditional voice taken by the story-teller. Your students will already know it from fairy tales: "Once upon a time there were three little pigs . . ." In contrast, the first-person point of view is used for personal memoirs. The narrator is involved in the story, not just observing it. A majority of young-adult novels are written in first-person, and so are some modern fairy tales, like Jon Scieszka's *The True Story of the Three Little Pigs*: "I'm the wolf. Alexander T. Wolf. You can call me Al."

Many students will cheerfully shift from one point of view to another, but real storytelling involves a choice on how the story is to be told. In general, the third-person point of view is best for traditional tales, adventure stories, mystery stories or any tale that involves different locations. The first-person point of view is more immediate and works best for stories where the emotional state of the narrator is an important factor.

We could explain this to our students, but we suspect that such theoretical issues would go sailing over their young heads. All that kids really need at this stage is some awareness of the narrative voice and consistency in its use.

 MINI-LESSON: *Teaching Point of View*

Go back to the "Practising Dialogue" mini-lesson and follow the same procedure: act out a scene and record the dialogue. Then *assign* a point of view. "All the girls will write as if they were Corey; all the boys will write as if they were Andrew." Give them a sentence to start them off, for example: "Girls, you begin with, 'I was just watching TV when Andrew came to the door holding my bike's handlebars.' Boys, you start with, 'I guess I shouldn't have left Corey's bike behind my dad's truck.'"

This exercise will show students how the same story becomes very different depending on the perspective of the narrator.

Next, ask students to adopt the third-person point of view. Remind them that this narrator sees both sides of the issue and can reveal what really happened. Start them off: "Andrew wasn't thinking when he left Corey's bike in the driveway."

Then compare the different points of view for this one event.

Elaborate the middle

The middle of the story consists of a series of events leading up to the climax, or high point. Now that the writer has grabbed the reader's interest with an engaging lead, she must keep that interest by creating anticipation. Is the protagonist going to solve his problem? If so, how will it be done?

A literary rule of thumb is to have three events leading up to the climax or three obstacles that get in the way of the main character achieving his goal. The Three Bears discover the porridge, the broken chair and then Goldilocks in the bed (and there are three bowls, chairs and beds, of course). "The Three Little Pigs" wouldn't have been much of a story if the first pig had built his house of bricks. The "magic of three" builds suspense and keeps the reader engaged.

 MINI-LESSON: *The "Magic of Three"*

We can use the "magic of three" to set up three hints leading to a discovery, or three events leading to the resolution of a problem, or three challenges that lead to the achievement of the main character's goal. The story organizers at the back of this chapter will help students outline these events.

Here are five situations to which your students can add obstacles. Model first, then have your students work in pairs to select a scenario and create three events.

- Pirate ➤ burying treasure
- Kids in haunted house ➤ seeing the ghost
- Princess meets dragon ➤ dragon lies dead
- Prince is trapped ➤ prince is freed
- Shy boy ➤ getting a date

You can easily cover your boards with the creative ways kids can elaborate on the middle of these stories.

Craft an effective ending

The problem is resolved, the challenge is met, the character has grown as a result of his experience. Now it's time to finish off the story in a way that leaves the reader satisfied, and perhaps a bit wiser.

One of the most effective ways to end a story is to revisit the opening paragraph and thereby make a circle. Other techniques include revealing the character's feelings or stating a decision or action:

- Jake promised to buy himself an alarm clock so he wouldn't be late again.
- He would never forget the time he met Wayne Gretzky.

As always, the more we look at successful published fiction, the more our students will understand about how to craft effective endings.

 MINI-LESSON: *Circular Conclusions*

Take your students to the library for a literary scavenger hunt. Tell them to scour the picture-book shelves for endings that echo the openings of their stories. To start, you can show them examples such as these:

> "Once upon a time, there was a cowboy bootmaker who was so poor even his shadow had holes in it."
>
> "And the boots that he made from leather and dreams were the best in the whole wide West."
>
> From *The Bootmaker and the Elves* by Susan Lowell

> "The way to start a day is this: Go outside and face the east and greet the sun with some kind of blessing or chant or song that you made yourself and keep for early morning."
>
> "And that's the way to start a day."
>
> From *The Way to Start a Day* by Byrd Baylor

> "There is no lake at Camp Green Lake."
>
> "Behind them, the sky had turned dark, and for the first time in over a hundred years, a drop of rain fell into the empty lake."
>
> From *Holes* by Louis Sachar

When they have found a good example (and checked it with you), have them write the opening sentence on a strip of colored paper and the concluding sentence on a strip of paper with a different color.

Play a matching game by distributing one colored strip to each student. You can ask the students to take turns reading aloud a lead sentence, then having the person with the matching conclusion reading hers aloud. Or, you can risk pandemonium and have the kids circulate, standing together when they find a match. However you do it, the point of matching beginnings and endings will have been made.

Revising

Don't forget TAG.

The TAG conference is an effective way to determine whether the story makes sense to the reader. The questions asked in a peer conference can identify points of confusion or unnecessary details.

Careful planning and drafting can lead to a story with its content well in place. If so, the writer will be able to focus on craft and style in the revision stage.

Of all the genres, the fictional narrative lends itself best to descriptive language and elaborative detail. Mini-lessons and required revision may focus on strong verbs, descriptive passages for setting or characters, effective dialogue and sentence variation.

Simply hearing their own stories read aloud sometimes enables writers to identify problems in their own compositions. TAG conferences (see pages 16–17) can help students identify gaps or points where interest lags. Ultimately, this is where your advice is most helpful. As an experienced reader, you can often suggest the major changes that will help a story develop through the revision stage.

Take time to conference with students at this stage of development. We suggest that you read the piece of writing on your own time and make a few notes to yourself to share with the student. Focus on only one or two elements. That's all the student will be able to take in at one time. Be prepared to offer specific, focused and constructive suggestions that will be "doable" by the student writer. And don't forget that simply starting over is a legitimate revision strategy – and may be the strategy of choice for a particular student. Only you know your students and what they need to improve their craft. Your job is not just to work with them to make this the best writing it can possibly be; it is to work with them to become the best writers they can be.

The Six Traits, as always, will be helpful in guiding discussion.

What an Effective Fictional Narrative Looks Like

Ideas	Organization	Voice	Word Choice	Sentence Fluency	Conventions
Story is based on a clearly developed character who experiences a problem that is satisfactorily resolved.	Beginning hooks the reader's attention. Story starts in the middle of the action. Episodes build anticipation. Conclusion wraps story up neatly.	Voice and style are suited to character and story. The best point of view for the story is used.	Word choice is creative and precise. Strong verbs move action along. Descriptive and figurative language adds interest.	Sentences are varied in length and style. Writing makes effective use of dialogue and questions. Some Very Short Sentences or fragments are used for effect.	Writing shows age- and risk-appropriate control of conventions.

 MINI-LESSON: *More "Magic of Three"*

We can also use the "magic of three" to craft effective sentences. We might have three subjects: "The students on the stage, the teachers in the wings, and the parents in the audience held their collective breaths when the main character forgot his lines." We might have three predicates: "The actor who played Hamlet took a gulp of air, gave his head a shake, and started the soliloquy over again." Or, we might have a sentence with three complete clauses: "The characters continued on with the play, the audience relaxed in their seats, and the teachers breathed a sigh of relief." After modeling some ways to craft sentences using the "magic of three," have the students insert a three-part sentence in one of their drafts.

Ernest Hemingway sharpened 20 pencils before writing. John Galsworthy required his wife to play piano nearby. Malcolm Lowry would rise early and go for a swim. Toni Morrison lights a candle before dawn and walks around the house.

 MINI-LESSON: *The Very Short Sentence*

The Very Short Sentence is a sentence or fragment of three to five words, used to add variety and effect. Show the students some examples of how they can use sentence fragments to add rhythm to their text. It might be an exclamation: "What a day!" It might involve repetition: "We waited. And waited. And waited." It might involve a contrast between a long sentence and a Very Short Sentence: "The actor paused at the end of his soliloquy, turned to the audience with a sigh and looked out to where his mother would have been sitting. At last, he cried."

The narrative genre is more forgiving than more formal text forms in allowing language patterns that break grammatical rules. Invite the students to search through a reading passage for examples of Very Short Sentences.

After the lesson, have students work with their own drafts to insert at least two Very Short Sentences.

 MINI-LESSON: *Strong Verbs*

Well-chosen verbs are one of the foundations of powerful writing. Two texts for helping to teach and reinforce verbs are the poem "The Turkey Shot out of the Oven" by Jack Prelutsky (from *It's Thanksgiving*) and the book *To Root, to Toot, to Parachute* by Brian P. Cleary. We suggest you read such texts to the class and highlight the verbs, discussing how the authors' vivid verbs help make their writing come alive.

It has been said that if you have to use an adverb, you haven't used a strong enough verb. Work with students to brainstorm lists of powerful verbs to replace worn-out verb-adverb phrases such as

> *walked slowly (trudged, ambled, loped, wandered)*
> *talked loudly*
> *slept soundly*

Put these lists on class charts that may be used as references for writing.

Editing and Publishing

The editing process is only necessary if the work is going to be published. As always, plan your mini-lessons around the needs of the students. Many books and other resources are available to help you plan instruction in grammar and conventions.

Word processors do much to deal with spelling problems and sometimes point to where grammar issues may lie, but they do little to fix problems in dialogue or paragraphing. Often it's helpful for students to read their work aloud to another student or a parent, so they can hear any problems on the page. Sometimes peer editing will help catch errors, though this can become quite onerous for the handful of kids in your class who have really good proofreading skills. Ultimately, your students are responsible for the quality of the work they want to publish. If many eyes will be looking at those works, though, better give them a good proofread yourself.

When they're ready, have the students recopy or word-process their stories, bearing in mind that many types of errors elude the spell checker. Remind them that real-world publishers always demand double-spacing of lines, decent margins on all sides of the page, and page numbers at the bottom. Your students may want to format and add pictures, either hand drawn or computer generated, but explain that elaborate title pages are neither great art nor an important part of the writing.

Publishing the finished story is that glorious moment for which all authors wait. The story is done, the ink is freshly dried on the page, no unsettling reviews have arrived and dreams of a movie offer are swirling about the author's mind. Celebrate the moment.

A coffee house or authors' party is a great way to showcase each student's polished writing. Having such an event gives each of your kids a chance to read aloud a small section of their work to the applause of their fellow authors.

Many teachers keep a permanent writing bulletin board with a space for each student to display his most recently published work. Stories may be placed in the school library to be read by others; just be sure to include a Reader Response sheet for readers to offer positive comments about the story.

A few print publications and Internet sites accept student stories, and more than a few writing contests will come up during the school year. If two or three of the stories from your class are going to be sent to a contest, you have a great motivator to bring all your students' work to publishable status.

The Halloween Pumpkin
by Whitney, Grade 3

Once upon a time there was a pumpkin. It was a Halloween pumpkin. His name was George. He was a great pumpkin. But an evil witch named Uguna came and cast a spell on George. The spell was that George would turn into a pickle. That's just what happened. George turned into a pickle. When his sister Crystal came she cried, "Mommy! Daddy! Come here! George has turned into a PICKLE!"

"Oh, my, an evil witch has turned George into a pickle. What shall we do?"

"Hmmm . . . I know," said her mother. "I will . . . I mean, we will think up a spell and one of us will say it." That's just what they did. Until one day Crystal said, "I've got it! Maybe we can say this: Goggle moggle ree, turn back into a pumpkin now! That's what we'll do." That's just what they did. And guess what, it worked. From then on, Uguna never showed her face again.

Mystery of the Missing Grandma
by Tracy, Grade 5

My grandma is a nice old lady and I try to visit her every time I can. She is in a wheel chair. I like to push her to the mall and to restaurants. I like to tell her what is in and what is out.

One day I was walking through the mall with her. I saw a pair of designer jeans that I had to get a closer look at or I would die. So I left my grandma at the till.

I got back to her in about five minutes. The only problem was that she wasn't there! I ran out of the store and there she was rolling down the mall floor with a tall man dressed in black. I ran after them but he was too fast. I ran out of the mall and there they were jumping into a car. On the bumper it said "So long sucker!"

Then I lost my temper. It felt like there was steam coming out of my nose. I stamped half way home and then I saw the car. It stopped. I ran and made a leap for the car. I landed on the back. The car pulled over.

The man got out of the car and said, "What do you want, Kid?"

I said, "I want my grandma."

I looked in the car. It wasn't my grandma, in fact it was a grandpa. I slowly walked away. The man yelled, "You should be ashamed of yourself."

I walked calmly the rest of the way home. I walked up my driveway and I heard a soft voice crying my name. I woke up. It was just a dream. My grandma was at my house. She said, "Take me to the mall."

I said, "No way!"

Student Writing

My Dog Ate the Mailman
by Bobby, Grade 4

Chapter One

One day Evan went to feed his dog, Charley, because if he wasn't fed, he would eat anything. But when Evan got there with his friend Colin, Charley had blood on his teeth.

"What happened?" asked Colin.

"I don't know," said Evan.

When Colin went home to check on his dog, Willy, he saw that the mail hadn't come yet but his next door neighbour had his mail. When Colin arrived back at Evan's house, he said, "I think I know why Charley has blood on his teeth."

"Why?" asked Evan.

"I think your dog ate the mailman."

Chapter Two

The next day there was some blood on Willy. "What's going on?" asked Evan.

"I don't know," said Colin. "Hey, let's call Mr. Allen."

So they called, but they just got Mrs. Allen and she said that Mr. Allen hadn't come home last night.

"I have an aunt that's in the hospital so let's go and visit her," said Evan.

"Okay," said Colin.

When they got there, they noticed that Mr. Allen had signed in, so they went to see him. "Hi, Mr. Allen," said Colin.

"Hi boys," said Mr. Allen.

Then both boys started thinking . . . if Charley didn't eat Mr. Allen, then what was the blood on his teeth?

When they got to Evan's house, his sister came out and said, "Who's been in my fake blood?"

That's what happened.

No Peas for Me Please

by Brad, Grade 6

"What's wrong, dear?" Mom asked. "You haven't touched your peas."

"Randy told me that peas are the Jolly Green Giant's boogers," I replied.

"Randy! I told you not to fill your brother's head with trash!" Dad hollered.

"There's no problem with it. He eats his own boogers anyway." Randy chuckled, laughing at his lame joke.

"Randy Bruce, don't be lippy! Go to your room!" Mom said angrily. Randy ran up to his room. My mom's a nice person but, when she gets mad, RUN!

"Now," she settled down. "Do you like the peas I got at the new supermarket downtown?" Dad and I nodded, trying to keep a straight face. They actually tasted awful.

Hi, I am Danny Bruce, and get ready for the tale of a lifetime. It all started that night when my mother bought these new peas for dinner. Since then, nothing has been the same.

The next morning, I woke up, put on my robe, and walked down the hallway to the bathroom. I turned the knob, opened the door, and arrived at the mirror, and my heart almost stopped. What I saw was a head . . . a bald head!

I rubbed my eyes, looking up again. Still there. I couldn't believe it. I was twelve years old and losing hair! I just stood there in shock for a minute.

Suddenly, Randy ran into the bathroom gasping, "Mom and Dad are . . . " he stared at me . . . "bald." I wasn't the only one, thank goodness.

It was very strange. The three of us were bald, but Randy had a full head of hair. Mom and Dad said that I should just say that I shaved my head.

I continued that day normally. I emptied the dishwasher, cleaned my room and took out the garbage. That's the weird part. I was doing the garbage when I found the empty bag from the peas. Some big, bold letters jumped out at me. They read:

DO NOT COOK!

SIDE EFFECTS: BALDNESS

ANTIDOTE: VINEGAR, SOYA SAUCE, KETCHUP AND PICKLE JUICE

"Yuck." I made a face. "Oh, well," I thought, "It's worth it."

That afternoon I made the antidote. It was an ugly brown colour. I drank it all up and waited. An hour later it worked. I had my old hair back. I thought to myself, "Do you think I should tell Mom and Dad? Nah, they look kind of cute that way."

Student Writing

A Weedy Situation (excerpt)

by Alecia, Grade 8

Jamie woke up early. It was already quite hot, and he stuck his head in the water barrel outside the cottage door to cool off. He and his friends were off to Emma Lake to go canoeing for the day.

Before long, Jamie and Kathy were in a canoe, paddling across the lake. "Can you swim?" Jamie asked his paddling partner.

"No!" Kathy replied. "Can you?"

"Wonderfully in a pool, but I'm scared of unknown water depths, like this lake." Jamie said quickly. Kathy looked as if she wanted to laugh.

All of a sudden a big pontoon boat rushed by their canoe, tipping it. Neither Jamie nor Kathy had bothered to bring a life jacket. Both of them fell in the water.

Jamie immediately grabbed onto the canoe, but Kathy was petrified.

"JAMIE! Jamie, help! I can't swim!" she shrieked. Suddenly, Kathy went under.

Jamie dove under the water. The water was extremely murky, but he could see the blurry shape of Kathy's sinking body. He dove after her. The stringy weeds clung to his legs. "Yuck! Leeches!" he thought.

Kathy hit the muddy bottom. Thankful that the water wasn't too deep, Jamie reached her and grabbed her around the waist. He tried to push off the bottom, but a weed held him there, wrapped around his ankle. He was running out of air. He yanked with all his might and finally broke loose from the weed. He would burst if he didn't get air soon. Just a bit more.

Jamie's hand broke the surface of the water, followed by his head. He gasped for air. Kathy spluttered some water out of her mouth. She seemed to be all right.

With one arm dragging Kathy and the other trying to propel himself forward, Jamie finally reached their tipped canoe.

Plot Brainstorm

Use this organizer to generate some ideas for your story. Describe your character in one sentence and think of a goal he or she might strive for. Then, come up with at least two possible problems and two possible resolutions for each problem. They won't all be great. That's okay. Choose the one that works best for you.

Character's Name: _____

One Sentence Description: _____

		Possible Resolution #1
	Possible Problem #1	
Goal #1		Possible Resolution #2
	Possible Problem #2	Possible Resolution #1
		Possible Resolution #2

Character Outline

Basic Description:

_____ is a_____, _____ _____ who
    name   adjective   adjective   noun

_____.

What is the character's goal?	Why does this character want it?
What personality flaws might prevent the character from achieving this?	What might the character be willing to do to achieve this?
What does the character look like?	What kind of person is the character?
What is the character afraid of?	What does the character care about?
What are some of the character's likes and dislikes?	Other Key Information:

Story Outline

Main Character:	
Goal:	
Problem(s):	
Events Leading to Resolution of Problem:	
Climax of the Story:	
Resolution:	

Lead:	Conclusion:

Plot Staircase Organizer

Problem:

Episode/Event/Complication #1:

Episode/Event/Complication #2:

Episode/Event/Complication #3 (Climax):

Resolution:

Checklist for Fictional Narrative Writing

Product

❏ My lead hooks the reader's attention.

❏ I started "in the middle" of the action.

❏ I defined a strong central character with a problem or goal.

❏ I have at least one complication or obstacle for the main character to overcome.

❏ I maintained the same point of view throughout.

❏ I have at least one section of dialogue to help define the characters.

❏ I have at least five great verbs to energize the story.

❏ I have at least one Very Short Sentence on each page.

❏ I created an effective title.

❏ My conclusion wraps up the story well.

Process

❏ I made a pre-writing plan.

❏ I had a TAG conference with _____ and made at least one substantive revision.

❏ I corrected my mistakes in spelling, capitalization, punctuation and word usage.

6

Just the Facts, Ma'am – The Informational Report

An informational report is what we write to share knowledge about a topic that we know or that we have learned about. It is part of a genre known as expository writing, sometimes called nonfiction or information text. Professional writers call these works "articles," or sometimes "pieces" in the shorthand of journalism.

Just as there are many varieties of stories, so there are many kinds of informational reports. A poster about a school dance, a list of items in a catalogue and even a No Parking sign are also forms of expository writing. They all serve the purpose of giving information.

An informational report can take a variety of forms. It may be a comparison of two things or an explanation of how something came to be. It may be a traditional "hamburger" essay on a topic in history or science. More creatively, students might even use a story format or a combination of words, images and specialized layout to present the information.

INFORMATIONAL REPORT FRAMEWORK

Purpose
To give information about a topic

Organization

BEGINNING: Introduces the topic and gives an overview of the information to be presented
MIDDLE: Presents facts and details about the topic, organized in paragraphs
END: Summarizes the information and wraps up in some strong way

Language Features

❈ Usually has more formal, factual language and tone
❈ Often includes technical vocabulary
❈ Generally presented in the present tense
❈ Written in third-person
❈ Uses transitional words: for one thing, also, as well

Examples

Magazine article, brochure, textbook, essay, research paper

It is every bit as important to follow the writing process for informational writing as it is for narrative writing.

The Importance of Process in Informational Writing

The informational report is a familiar assignment for students throughout their school years. They write reports on topics in science, history, health and geography from first grade to graduation. All too often, however, we teachers abandon the writing process when we focus on teaching students to research and write information about a topic. Sometimes, we may teach students to collect information and to organize their ideas, but then leave them to their own devices to craft and revise the final product. At worst, we simply assign the topic and pay no more attention until the final product is handed in. We sometimes forget that the writing process is *not* the exclusive domain of the language arts program. We are all teachers of writing, regardless of the subject area.

So let us say in bold type: **It is every bit as important to use a planning-drafting-revising-editing-publishing process for informational writing as it is for narrative writing.** A report may be full of excellent information, but if it is not well written, it will not serve its purpose of informing and educating the reader. Taking time to teach students the structures and processes of informational writing will pay off with well-crafted reports that are full of voice and style as well as facts and details.

Teaching students how to write an informational report can also be integrated with content-area learning. You might want to take advantage of a unit in science or history to provide explicit modeling and guided practice in the elements of writing an informational report. But it is every bit as valid to make informational writing part of the language arts program.

Strategies for Reading Nonfiction Texts

Reading nonfiction texts should already be a part of the elementary language arts curriculum. Take advantage of the opportunity to link language arts with content-area subjects by *taking time to teach* students how to *read* textbooks and other informational texts. We sometimes forget that reading informational text requires all of the strategies needed for reading narrative text – and more!

Expository text presents unique challenges in that it is information-dense and contains vocabulary specific to the subject. It also provides supports, however, in the form of headings, graphics, bold and italicized typefaces. We can teach students to consciously look for and make use of these supports. Students will find informational text much more accessible when they know how to look for and use the supports built into the text. This knowledge will also provide them with tools and techniques for writing their own informational reports.

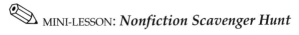 MINI-LESSON: *Nonfiction Scavenger Hunt*

Provide each group of students with a piece of informational writing; it can be the same text for each or completely different books for various groups. Have them search for all of the features of the text that help them access the information in that book. Record the ideas on the chart. Your chart should include the following:

Headings and subheadings

Pictures with captions

Charts and graphs

Bold print

Italicized print

Table of Contents

Glossary

Index

Transition words: such as, for example, in contrast to

Small "chunks" of text

After you've identified these aspects of nonfiction text, take time to teach them so students know how to use these supports. Have them practise using an index or glossary and explicitly teach the use of graphics such as charts and pictures. Encourage students to get in the habit of previewing a text before reading it. A quick look at the headings, pictures and graphics can establish a context for reading and facilitate comprehension.

You might use *Beaks!* and other informational picture books by Sneed B. Collard III as excellent models for generalities and specific facts. Each page begins with a topic sentence in large, bold print. The rest of the page contains interesting details to support that statement.

Read, read, read!

Now it's time to take advantage of some of those supports by reading a variety of nonfiction texts. Sometimes it's hard to decide what to write about until you've done a little reading on the subject. Pre-reading gives the writer enough background information to define and refine his subject.

You should have no problem finding terrific nonfiction texts to use as models. Information books for kids have become a booming business for publishers in recent years. A search in the library catalogue or an online bookstore will yield many titles on just about any topic of interest. Junior magazines, such as *Owl, Ranger Rick* or *National Geographic Kids,* are also great sources for informational reading.

The problem with most informational text is that it assumes the reader has some background knowledge about the topic. So, before reading, it's a good idea for students to ask themselves: *What do I already know about this topic?* Next, it is useful to set a purpose for reading: *What do I hope to learn from this reading?* Then, as they read, they should be thinking, *What am I learning?*

The K-W-L-S chart is an adaptation of our friend Donna Ogle's classic K-W-L strategy. It provides a structure for thinking about nonfiction text, both before and after reading: **K** = What I **K**now; **W** = What I **W**ant to find out; **L** = What I've **L**earned; **S** = What I **S**till want to learn.

Before reading, the student outlines what she already knows about the topic, thereby accessing prior knowledge and vocabulary. She then sets a purpose for reading by articulating what she hopes or thinks she will learn. *During and after* reading, the reader takes note of what she is learning about the topic, then thinks about what questions were unanswered or what new questions the reading raised.

 MINI-LESSON: *Teaching the K-W-L-S Organizer*

Choose a topic based on one of your themes or units of study, such as the moon. Prepare a page of informational text on that topic and a large chart divided into four sections. (See "K-W-L-S" on page 106.)

Invite students to share facts that they already know about the moon. Note these in the "K" section. Together with the students, develop a list of questions they have about the moon. Write these in the "W" section.

If the text is easily readable by all students, have them read it independently; if it is difficult for many students, you may want to read it aloud. After reading, invite the students to share facts that they learned from the reading, and record them in the "L" section. Together, note any questions that were not answered or new questions that the students raise in the "S" section.

Practise using this strategy in groups before expecting students to use it on their own. Remember that the purpose of this activity is to teach students a strategy for reading informational text. It is a starting point for gathering information about a topic.

Pre-writing

Most writers agree that this is the most important – and time-consuming – part of the writing process. Ask any journalist and you'll get the same answer: it can take hours or entire days to find and verify information that ultimately takes up only a few column inches of space. That's real information writing.

In school report writing, it is during the pre-writing stage that the writer must define and refine his topic, determine research questions and gather the information that will comprise the content of the piece. Students need to be supported in each of these activities.

Narrow the topic

Choosing a topic can be difficult for many writers, regardless of the genre. The trick is to determine, ahead of time, how specific the report can be. One mistake students make in report writing is choosing a topic that is too general, such as Canada, Dinosaurs, or Space. Researching

If you write the ideas on sticky notes rather than right on the chart, they can be moved, manipulated, and sorted later.

the topic can be overwhelming and the report becomes vague. How often have we daydreamed during a student report on Florida when it would have been much more interesting and manageable – for both writer and reader – to read "Great Places to Visit in Florida" or "Rocket Launching at Cape Canaveral"? On the other hand, if students choose a topic that is too specific, it may be difficult to find enough research material. Using an organizer can help them refine the topic, define the research questions and outline the text.

 MINI-LESSON: *Using an Organizer to Refine a Topic*

Use the Topic Tree organizer on page 107 to demonstrate to students how they might take a general topic and make it more specific.

Together, take a large topic, such as Space, then break it down into two smaller topics, and then divide each of them into three smaller topics. Talk with the students about the level of specificity they should choose when writing a report. When you are ready to assign the report, give the students a general topic and have them create their own Topic Tree charts to find the areas of interest that they want to research.

Once the topic is in place, there's one more step before students can start gathering information. Student (and many adult) writers need guidelines for their research. Outlining a series of questions or subtopics helps students focus their research and weed out unnecessary information. For students in the middle grades, four or five research questions or subtopics are adequate. "Other Interesting Facts" is a useful addition for most research topics.

Internet Issues

Cut-and-paste makes it all too easy for students to hit a few Web sites and then paste together a report from the fragments they find. Some colleges now pay search services to check papers for plagiarism, but it's important to teach real research early – before bad habits develop.

Find reference materials

Many technologically oriented students find it hard to believe there are sources of information other than the Internet. How naïve they are! Although the Internet is useful and convenient, there is an absence of control on the accuracy of information it presents. This lack is only one reason that our students need to be made aware that other sources of information are out there.

Another challenge the Internet presents is to ensure that students clearly understand the difference between facts and opinions. You may want to spend some time reading texts to distinguish the two. Contrast a news article and an editorial on the same topic, for instance, so your students can see how they differ.

 MINI-LESSON: *Finding References*

Together with your students, make a list of all of the sources they might use to find information about their topic. Make sure you include books, encyclopedias, newspapers, almanacs, magazines and brochures, not to mention people-experts on the topic (see page 131). Emphasize that the Internet is only one source. Divide the list up among pairs of students and send each on a "treasure hunt" to find a sample of that source.

MINI-LESSON: *The "Gathering Grid"*

Using a "Gathering Grid" sheet (see page 108), list three key resources on a topic across the top. (Tell older students that you expect more than three.) We suggest that you require three different *types* of resources: for example, a Web site, a book and a magazine article. Next, show how to list research questions or subtopics down the side. The remaining blocks are for collecting information. Model this for the students, then guide them through the process themselves.

As students do their research, teach them how to write a simple bibliography. Even the youngest students should be able to note at least the title, author and copyright date.

Practise note-taking.

Note-taking needs practice just like any other activity. Give the students a one-page article to distill into point-form notes. Read an article aloud and have them take notes as you read. Give them three Internet pieces and have them judge which is most useful and most reliable while they take notes.

Take notes

Effective note-taking is another important strategy. Students must learn to discern key words and ideas, and to gather information without plagiarism. Once again, demonstration and modeling, followed by plenty of guided practice, are essential to ensure that students grasp the concept of taking notes. Note-taking will be a valuable skill, both in school and in the larger school of life.

Only after students have had plenty of time to practise note-taking should they be expected to conduct their own research. By this point, your students should have defined and refined their topic, generated some research questions, found reference materials and gathered information. When time and care are taken in this pre-writing stage, the rest of the writing process will be much easier.

 MINI-LESSON: *"Telegram Notes"*

Tell students you are taking them back in time to the days when people sent information via telegram. Because telegrams cost money for each word, people had to convey their messages using as few words as possible. When we take notes, we operate on the same principle: we need just enough words to help us recall the key ideas, without any extra information.

Provide each student with a photocopied page of information – a page from a history textbook will work. Then tell the kids to focus on one sentence at a time by putting a slash mark at the end of each sentence. Read the sentence and, together, decide whether it answers any of the research questions about the topic. If it does not provide any relevant information, go on to the next sentence, putting a slash mark at the end of it. When you encounter some relevant information, underline or highlight any key words in the sentence. Then create a jot note that gives the relevant information as briefly as possible. Be careful that you're not too thrifty with the words, though; your notes have to mean something to you when you read them later.

Methodically read through the whole text in this way, teaching students to be conscious of whether the information addresses their topics and to record facts in a manner that is economical but useful.

Organize time

Not every piece of informational writing is a lengthy work, but some may be. The longer the piece, the more your students will need help in organizing their time for research, pre-writing, drafting, revision and editing. The "Organizing Your Time" chart on page 109 can be filled out at the beginning of a long assignment so students can see the writing as a set of manageable steps. One big difference between professional writers and amateurs is in time management: professionals plan the steps to get one job done and then move on; amateurs can dither for years. Why not teach your students professional techniques early on?

Drafting

Paul: I think the hamburger paragraph is overused and you won't find a succession of burger paragraphs in the writing of Montaigne or Pierre Berton.

Lori: It may seem overused to you, but it's still a good starting point for some kids.

There is one more lesson that you may want to teach before your students go any further: how to write an expository paragraph. These paragraphs almost always have a topic sentence, frequently the first sentence (though the topic sentence may show up in other places in highly crafted professional writing). Once again, the best teaching will involve reading expository paragraphs and highlighting topic sentences. Demonstrate to students that the purpose of the topic sentence is to give an overview of what the paragraph is about; it offers a general statement, with the rest of the paragraph containing supporting detail.

Student can use Gathering Grids to write one paragraph for each of the topics. It may be necessary to model the process of converting jot notes into complete sentences and paragraphs. Emphasize the importance of beginning each paragraph with an effective topic sentence and adding relevant details later. Depending on the maturity of the students and the nature of the topic, encourage them to write at least three detail sentences per paragraph.

You have probably encountered the metaphor of a hamburger paragraph, with the top and bottom halves of the bun relating to the opening and closing sentences in the paragraph. The meat and condiments become the details in the middle. A savory analogy, no doubt, but often the summary sentence can make the writing sound stilted and affected. Moreover, the meat will often be bigger than the bun, leading to a wacky metaphor indeed. We recommend saving the hamburger concept for very long paragraphs in which the main idea might have been lost in a mire of detail. Perhaps better yet, break up overly long paragraphs into two or three of more manageable size.

 MINI-LESSON: *Creating Interesting Topic Sentences*

Teach students that topic sentences may take different forms. Here are some common forms with examples:

- Generalizations: *"There are two types of terrain on the moon."*
- Personal statements: *"It is fascinating to think about the effects of the gravitational forces between Earth and moon."*

- Questions: *"Do you remember where you were on July 20, 1969? Probably gathered around your television set, watching astronauts walk on the moon."*
- Connections with the reader: *"You may be surprised to know that the moon is sometimes referred to as a "terrestrial planet."*

The least effective form of topic sentence is "I am going to tell you about . . ." It should be banished from your classroom. To emphasize this, have students work in pairs or small groups with the essay "The Black Widow" (see page 103) to revise the topic sentence in each paragraph.

Revising

When the students' drafts are complete, you may want to have them participate in TAG conferences, with partners, to work on developing clarity and style. Use the following chart to look for areas that may be improved in your students' writing:

What Effective Informational Writing Looks Like

Ideas	Organization	Voice	Word Choice	Sentence Fluency	Conventions
There is a clear focus to the writing. All details enhance the main idea. The writing covers the topic thoroughly.	All details about a topic are in the same paragraph. The opening paragraph hooks the readers' attention and gives an overview. The closing paragraph summarizes the topic and wraps up the report neatly.	Although the writing is informational, it has personality and appropriate style. It engages the reader.	Words are carefully chosen to convey the intended information. There is no unnecessary repetition of words.	Sentences are varied in structure. The flow is logical and smooth.	Spelling and mechanics are appropriate for the level of the writer.

MINI-LESSON: *Introductions and Conclusions – The Bread for the Sandwich*

Use a visual demonstration for this lesson. Tell students you are going to make a sandwich. Get out some meat, some cheese and some tomatoes. Spread a little mustard and mayo on top and get ready to eat. Inevitably, someone will comment that a sandwich also needs bread – the top and bottom of the sandwich – to hold it together.

In the same way, the introductory paragraph and concluding paragraph hold the report together. The opening sentence should hook the reader's attention and the remainder of the paragraph give an overview of what the report will contain. The closing paragraph summarizes the preceding information and ends neatly with a wrap-up sentence.

Concluding sentences might begin in these ways:

- "As you can see, . . . "
- "It is clear that . . . "
- "I'm sure you will agree . . . "
- "All in all, . . . "

It's always a good idea to follow up with samples of effective introductions and conclusions for students to read. In truth, many of your students will not have written introductory paragraphs yet, so part of this lesson will be to draft introductions and conclusions for their reports.

 MINI-LESSON: *Adding Voice and Style with "Gold Nuggets"*

During the days of the gold rush, a prospector would be thrilled to find gleaming chunks of gold among the rocks. In the same way, a reader is engaged by "gold nuggets" in a piece of informational writing. We use the term to refer to statements that add interest and voice to a piece of writing. What makes a gold nugget?

- an interesting quote
- statistics
- an anecdote
- a Very Short Sentence (see page 82)
- an amazing fact

- a colorful description
- an unusual comparison
- a personal connection
- a question
- a joke or something funny

Work together on a common text to try out different types of gold nuggets. Read them aloud and talk about whether they enhance or detract from the text. Then have students work on adding one or two gold nuggets to their own reports.

 MINI-LESSON: *Avoiding Useless, Ineffectual and Unnecessary Repetition*

How do you write a report on the moon without using the word "moon" over and over and over? A research report must, of necessity, make frequent references to the same topic or word. Encourage students to generate a list of alternative terms for their topic of choice. For example, synonymous words and phrases for the moon might include these: "Earth's natural satellite," "our nearest neighbor in space," or "a lunar body." Rule of thumb: Have students highlight each reference to their topic and replace every third reference with a synonymous phrase.

Does report writing have "voice"?

You bet it does. No one would ever confuse Bill Bryson with Christie Blatchford – the voice is too different. Information writing can have lots of voice – with or without using the word "I." Look at the samples on pages 103 to 105 for information writing with and without voice.

Editing and Publishing

All reports must be edited for mistakes in conventions before they are published. Students should be encouraged to edit their own work, but the teacher should always be the final editor, to ensure that all is correct.

Mini-lessons on editing should be determined by the kinds of mistakes made by the students. Focus on one or two key issues.

Kids often have problems in predictable areas:

- where to paragraph
- how to use commas properly
- how to avoid run-on sentences
- what to capitalize

Other problems might be more specific to the topic, the kind of writing, or the sophistication of your students:

- semi-colon versus period
- effective graphics
- footnotes and bibliography
- quotes from other sources
- plagiarism versus "your own words"

Once all these problems have been resolved, students are ready to publish their work. Reports can be published in many ways: as a page of text, as a picture book, as a brochure or as a newsletter. As your students get ready to publish, revisit the list of features of informational writing that you prepared with them at the outset of this assignment.

Students may wish to add graphics, headings, font variations and other elements. Teach the students to take advantage of the computer as an efficient publishing tool. You may even require certain elements, such as the insertion of some graphics and at least two subheadings. See some of the exercises in Chapter 8 on procedural writing to help in adding graphics to word-processed text.

Teaching students how to write an informational report does not occur overnight. But taking the time to teach each stage of the process will provide students with a repertoire of tools that will be useful throughout school and life.

The Black Widow
by Jamie, Grade 4

I am going to tell you about the Black Widow. First I am going to tell you about where it lives. It lives in certain places in North America and Australia. That is where the black widow lives.

Now I am going to tell you what it looks like or another word for it is description. It is black except for these three dots on its belly. It is really big and has long legs. That is all I can really tell you about what it looks like.

I am going to tell you about what it does or another word for it is habits. They do not like to bite or fight. If they are disturbed they might strike. Something kind of interesting is that it glues its egg sac to a branch. That is all I can tell you about what a Black Widow does.

Finally the interesting facts. The Black Widow is poisonous to people. The false Black Widow is harmless though. Did you know that the female is bigger than the male? Did you know also that the female bites? If you didn't, well you do now. That is the end of my interesting facts and my report on the Black Widow. I hope you liked it!

Pluto: The Tiny Planet
by Terri, Grade 6

Pluto is an interesting planet. It is tiny and believed to be blue! How far is it? What is it made of? Who discovered it, men or women? Let's find out.

I can't see it! Pluto is so far from the Earth it has to be seen by a telescope. Pluto is approximately 3,670 million km from the Sun. It takes Pluto 248 years to travel around the sun once. Pluto can pass Neptune every 20 years.

It's freezing up here! Pluto is so cold and icy because it is so far from the sun. Pluto's one moon, Charon, is half the size of its tiny planet friend. Pluto is rocky at the core and below that is frozen water.

I've found it! Clyde W. Tombaugh was born in 1906. On March 13, 1930, Tombaugh discovered Pluto. He took three wonderful photos.

I forgot! Pluto is so far away you need a telescope to find it. It's so cold that if you sat down, you'd probably be stuck there. It would be so neat to see Pluto in a rocket.

Some day I hope people do go to Pluto and see it.

Bees
by Jessica, Grade 5

Bees

Did you know there are 20,000 kinds of bees? Bees are insects. Bees are either a queen, worker or a drone. There are social bees and solitary bees.

Appearance

There are many colours of bees like black, yellow, brown, green and blue. They have three body parts. The head, which has the eyes and the antenna, the thorax which has the wings and legs, and the abdomen which has the stinger. Bees also have hair on their eyes and legs.

Diet

Bees use a proboscis (a tube-like tongue) for drinking nectar. They drink nectar and eat the pollen that comes from flowers. Worker bees use nectar and pollen to make honey and feed the young. Worker bees help pollinate flowers. The hair on their legs carries the pollen and the pouches on the legs also carry the pollen.

Habitat

Solitary bees build their nests in trees, plants or on the ground. Social bees build hives out of beeswax and they make the beeswax in their own bodies. Did you know there are about 50,000 bees in each hive?

Enemies

Bears eat the honey bees make. Some toads, spiders and birds eat bees. The bees sting to protect themselves. After they sting, the stinger breaks off and the bee dies.

Life Stages

Bees have four life stages. First the queen lays an egg. In the second stage the egg turns into a larva. The larva turns into a pupa and then into an adult. The queen mates the drone. After the drone is done mating it dies. Social queen bees lay up to 1500 eggs a day.

Interesting Facts

Bees communicate by scent and doing some kind of dance. In the winter or on a chilly day, they huddle and vibrate to keep warm.

I think bees are very neat. I would like to be a beekeeper.

Student Writing

Bows and Arrows, to the Point
by Christine, Grade 7

Twang, plunk, bulls eye! From early times, around 25,000 years ago, humans in many places all over the world have used the bow and arrow. This piercing, ranged or distance weapon has been used in war and is still occasionally used for hunting, competitions or just for recreational target shooting. Although mostly replaced by guns and other military weapons, people still like to use the bow and arrow for the old-fashioned charms it seems to possess.

Simple? Not quite. The make-up of a bow seems simple enough, considering it consists of only two main parts, but, of course, things aren't always what they seem. The bow itself is a curved piece of wood, metal or plastic that is grasped by the bowman. This part is most commonly made from a special kind of wood called yew, found in Spain, Italy and western parts of America. It can be made of ash as well, because it must be a wood that bends. In the centre of the bow, it might have a place to rest your arrow on, but most commonly it only has a grip for the archer to hold onto. The string is attached at either end of the bow, at the top and the bottom. The string of the bow has been made from many things throughout time, from bison sinew to other dried animal parts such as intestines or hair.

The arrows are normally made from spruce, Norway pine or certain kinds of cedar. They range in length from 60 to 70 cm, depending on whether the bowman is male or female. At the front of the arrow is the pointed tip, or arrowhead, usually made from steel today but made from flint or bone in the past. At the end of the arrow, feathers are placed so that the arrow will fly straighter and true to the target. This is called the nock.

Bows and arrows aren't only for the male selection of our planet. A man's bow is about two metres long and takes the strength to pull 15 to 30 kg to draw it back. A woman's bow, which of course is a bit smaller, is less than two metres long. It takes the strength only to pull 7 to 15 kg. The amount of strength required has been reduced by extra strings and cables that make it easier to pull. Many people still treasure the use of this weapon, therefore, proving that archery should be around for a while yet.

K – W – L – S

Before Reading	
What I Already <u>K</u>now	What I <u>W</u>ant to Learn

After Reading	
What I <u>L</u>earned	What I <u>S</u>till Want to Know

Topic Tree

Put your biggest idea in the box at the base of the tree. Break it into two smaller ideas in the branches. Then divide each of those into three ideas at the treetop.

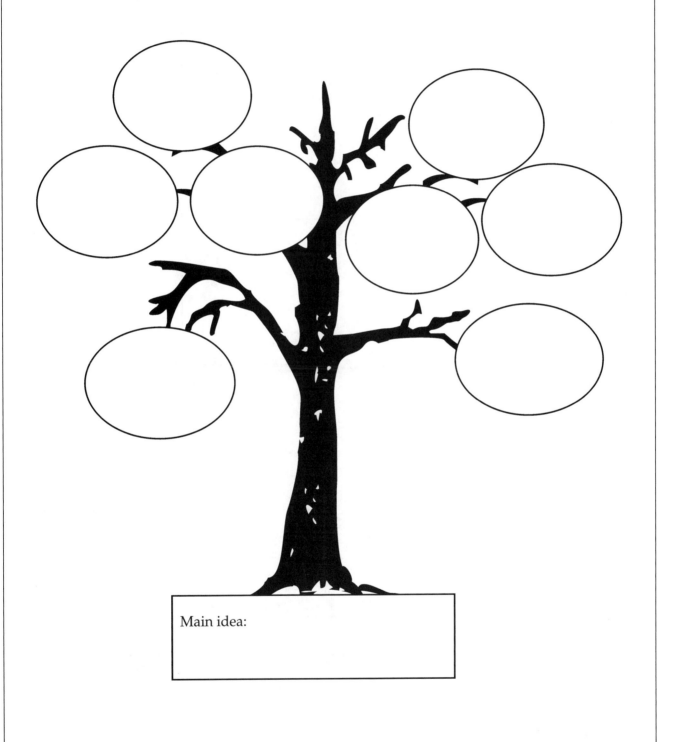

Main idea:

Gathering Grid

Main topic:	Resource 1	Resource 2	Resource 3
Subtopic or question			
Subtopic or question			
Subtopic or question			
Subtopic or question			

Organizing Your Time

Stage of the Project	Deadline
1. Defining and refining the topic	
2. Generating research questions	
3. Collecting notes	
4. Making the first draft	
5. Revising	
6. Self-editing	
7. Publishing	

Organizing Your Time

Stage of the Project	Deadline
1. Defining and refining the topic	
2. Generating research questions	
3. Collecting notes	
4. Making the first draft	
5. Revising	
6. Self-editing	
7. Publishing	

Adding Voice and Style with Gold Nuggets

You can make your text more interesting to readers by including some of these gold nuggets:

- **an interesting quote**

- **a number or statistic**

- **a brief anecdote**

- **an amazing fact**

- **a Very Short Sentence**

- **a colorful description**

- **an unusual comparison**

- **a question**

- **something funny**

- **a personal connection**

7

What Do They Really Think? – The Opinion Piece

Persuasive writing is intended to convey an opinion in a powerful way. When done well – consider Marc Antony's "Friends, Romans, Countrymen" speech – such works can convince others to actively support the author's view. When done poorly, important actions can be left undone and the person promoting an idea looked upon with disrespect.

That's why even the youngest students should know how to state an opinion and provide support. What is your favorite time of year and why? Why did you like that book? What do you want for Christmas and why should your parents spend that much money on something that will break in two days? For older students, persuasive writing becomes a fairly sophisticated form because it requires the author to direct his writing to a particular audience and to do so with considerable effect. The best persuasive writing not only offers cogent arguments, it anticipates possible contrary opinions and refutes those ideas, thereby bolstering its own strength. This is the kind of writing we see in newspaper editorials, political writing, speeches and legal defences. You might say that persuasive writing is the very basis of democracy: it inspires clear thinking, well-supported opinions and logical responses.

Effective persuasive writing states a clear opinion on an issue, then uses facts, examples and reasons to support the opinion. Generally it has three sections: an introduction, which provides an opinion and gets the reader involved in the argument; a body, which contains facts and reasons to support the opinion; and a conclusion, which restates the opinion, urges the reader to take action and usually makes a positive statement.

The opinion piece is an essential tool for dealing with the challenges of day-to-day life. Every time we write a letter of complaint, make a request or share a passionate opinion, we are engaging in persuasive writing. That's why it is so important that students learn to write well in this genre.

Purpose	**Organization**
To give an opinion; to persuade or convince an audience	THESIS: States point of view or position and provides background information ARGUMENT: Provides support for position; may anticipate opposite point of view and counteract CONCLUSION: Summarizes key points and redefines or reviews initial position

Language Features

* ❊ Addressed to a specific audience
* ❊ May be in first-person (I), second-person (you) or third-person (they)
* ❊ Has clear organization
* ❊ Uses transitional words to indicate order: *first, for one thing, also*
* ❊ Uses persuasive verbs: *should, need, must*
* ❊ Makes logical arguments with solid support
* ❊ Has knowledgeable and passionate voice
* ❊ Includes persuasive rhetorical devices to bolster argument

Examples

Essays, editorials, speeches, advertisements, opinion pieces, debates, court arguments, political views

Understanding What's Fact and What's Opinion

A **fact** is a statement that can be proved.

An **opinion** is a statement that cannot be proved. It describes how a person feels about something.

Encourage your students to read many examples of persuasive or opinion writing. Look for samples in the newspaper and save examples from previous classes to share with your students before they begin to write.

One key understanding that writers need before they can have success with persuasive writing is the difference between fact and opinion. Young students (and even some adults) have difficulty with this. So, when you read examples of published and student opinion pieces, pay attention to opinions and facts. Use two different high-lighters, marking opinions with one color and facts with the other.

It should not be hard for students to identify persuasive writing, especially after they have had many opportunities to read published and student examples. Choose one particularly effective piece of persuasive writing and have the students note as many elements of persuasive rhetoric and writer's craft as they can find.

Be sure to check out these picture books and others for teaching persuasive writing:

My Brother Dan's Delicious by Steven Layne
My Name Is Jorge, On Both Sides of the River by Jane Medina
Earrings by Judith Viorst
Dear Mrs. LaRue: Letters from Obedience School by Mark Teague
Glasses: Who Needs 'Em? by Jon Scieszka
Should There Be Zoos? by Tony Stead
"One Sister for Sale" by Shel Silverstein

As a debating coach, Paul likes to set up easy debates so that students can practise reasoning skills. For instance: *Resolved: That students at our school should wear uniforms.* Kids work in teams of three to assemble their arguments. Ultimately, this exercise can lead to real debates on many issues.

Taking a Position

Even before you get the kids to begin a real piece of persuasive writing, have them practise "giving reasons." A common weakness of student writing is unsubstantiated opinions or generalized ideas without support. By practising rational argument, your students will be better able to write effectively. Here are three activities to help students practise defending a position or idea.

 MINI-LESSON: *The Secret Knowledge of Grown-ups*

Read *The Secret Knowledge of Grown-ups*, the 1997 Caldecott Medal–winning picture book by David Wisniewski. The book offers fantastic "real" reasons for common rules that parents make. Students will have great fun listening to the "real" reason you should eat your vegetables or not jump on the bed. Then brainstorm a list of common household or school rules and have students invent the "real" reasons for these rules.

 MINI-LESSON: *"Fairy Tale Academy Awards"*

One way to help students understand the concept of perspective, or point of view, is to have them take on the role of a familiar fairy-tale character. Having fairy-tale villains, such as the giant in "Jack in the Beanstalk" or the witch in "Hansel and Gretel," defend their own actions helps young writers see other perspectives.

Then have the class vote for such "Honors" as the scariest, the luckiest, the greediest, the smartest. Ask students to write a paragraph nominating a character for the award and providing reasons for the nomination. Or, have them write an acceptance speech from the perspective of the character.

 MINI-LESSON: *Letters to Businesses*

A great way to introduce persuasive writing to students is to have them write letters to stores or other businesses where they have experienced exemplary service and businesses where they have not had a good experience.

With the students, brainstorm names of places where they like to eat, shop or go for entertainment. After each suggestion, have the students indicate why they liked that particular place.

Invite each student to select one place of business and freewrite for one page about personal experiences with that establishment. Encourage all students to include specific details, including sights, sounds and smells, as well as snippets of dialogue.

Allow students to meet in groups to share their stories. Often this oral sharing elicits ideas from other members of the group and may even remind a writer of additional ideas. Encourage them to add notes to their writing.

On another occasion, follow the same procedure with a negative experience from an eating, shopping or entertainment establishment. If the students can't think of a specific experience, they may be able to write about someone else's experience, or dissatisfaction with a particular product.

As you work through the elements of persuasive writing, your students should revise, edit and then mail one of their letters. But don't be frivolous. Remember that businesses tend to take this kind of mail very seriously. Your students are quite likely to receive a reply.

Techniques for Persuasion

While you're looking at the ways in which students can effectively persuade a reader, you have a chance to consider the emotional techniques so often used on television and in certain types of polemical writing. Kids will have fun – and develop media awareness – by looking for examples of these techniques when they watch TV commercials:

- **Loaded words:** These words and phrases have a strong emotional impact on the reader. "Mrs. Clean kills *deadly* germs, protecting the lives of your *loved ones*."
- **Endorsements:** A product is associated with a well-known person or person of authority. "Even Santa Claus drinks slim-fast shakes."
- **Expert opinion:** This statement comes from a person of knowledge or a recognized authority: "The Canadian Dental Association says that flossing can save your teeth."
- **Glittering generality:** This general, nonspecific assertion somehow connects a product with desirability. "New and Improved Kitty Snacks! Treat your cat to the best!"
- **Bandwagon appeal:** This general statement gives a sense that "everyone" agrees with a particular idea. "Nobody likes to sit at the table next to a smoker."
- **Phony statistics:** Statistics may be based on a small sample size or overgeneralized. "Three out of four dentists in Dallas preferred new Bogus Brand toothpaste."
- **Connection with the reader:** Writers often try to get the reader on-side by joining with the reader through a phrase or two, for example, "You and I both know . . . " or by asking the reader, "Can you believe that . . . ?"
- **Compliments or praise for the reader's intelligence:** Flattery can get a writer or TV copywriter far indeed. "New Snicky Snacks, made especially for you, the discerning snacker."

 MINI-LESSON: *Advertising Scavenger Hunt*

Bring in a collection of old magazines and send the students on a hunt for persuasion techniques in advertising. Have them cut out magazine advertisements and label the strategies they see. Display the ads on a bulletin board and discuss the impact of each.

Some Fun Topics

Not all persuasive pieces need to be serious. Try a few of these:

- Birthdays can be dangerous.
- Fire hydrants should be painted purple.
- The earth is really square.
- The tooth fairy is real.

Issues to Write About

After you've practised the basics of rational argument, it's time to brainstorm a list of issues the kids care about. These will range from personal issues such as "Should parents be able to divorce?" to global issues such as "Should medicines be tested on animals?" We've also included a list of age-appropriate topics on page 122 in case your students need some ideas.

 MINI-LESSON: *Topic Web*

One way to determine whether a topic will work for a persuasive essay is to create a "web of support." Begin by modeling the process for your students. You might use the topic web below as an example.

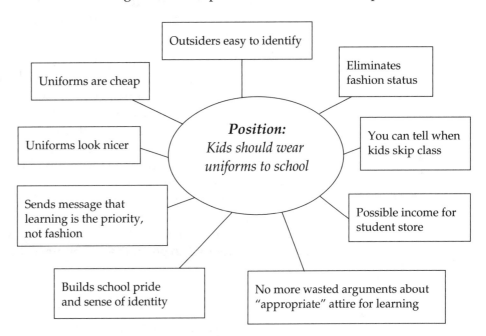

Ask each student or pair of students to choose one issue that they think they could write about. Have them brainstorm an ideas web for that issue (see "Facts and Reasons Organizer" on page 123). Remind them that the principles of brainstorming include writing every idea that comes to mind, without judgment. They can go back and evaluate the ideas later.

After they have brainstormed for ten minutes, have them put a star beside the top three or four ideas and number them 1, 2, 3 from strongest to weakest.

Repeat this webbing activity at least two more times to give students practice providing support for ideas and to generate material to work with when they are ready to begin writing. Suggest that they choose the issue they care most about and have supported most strongly.

Pre-writing

By this time, students have chosen their topic and brainstormed some supporting details. What comes next? Determining the audience and their purpose for writing.

Students have various questions to consider. Who is going to read this piece of writing: their teacher, their parents, the government, a businessperson, their friends? What do they hope to achieve with it? Do they simply want the audience to know about their opinion? Are they recommending some course of action, such as asking a store to provide them with a replacement for a defective product or persuading the principal to allow the class to run a bake sale?

The best way to get answers to these questions, and thereby focus student writing, is to use the RAFTS approach. You'll recall from Chapter 1 that the acronym RAFTS stands for **Role-Audience-Format-Topic-Strong verb**. It is an excellent planning tool for persuasive writing.

- *Role* refers to the perspective from which the writer is writing. Is the student an angry customer, a concerned citizen, a student council member? Is he personally involved with the issue, or is he speaking on behalf of a group or a principle?
- *Audience* refers to who will read the piece of writing. The style, tone and language of the piece is likely to vary according to the audience.
- *Format* is the form the writing will take: a letter to the editor, an essay, a speech?
- *Topic* is, obviously, what the writing is about. What is the issue that the writer is addressing?
- *Strong verb* refers to the purpose for writing. Opinion writing is intended to persuade, to convince, to call to action.

 MINI-LESSON: *RAFTS Statement*

Use the poster found on page 21 to review the RAFTS planner. Then have each student prepare a statement such as this:

> As _____, write a _____
> (role)   (format)
> _____ ing (to) _____
> (strong verb)   (audience)
> about _____.
> (topic)

Example: As a consumer, write a letter complaining to Acme Toy Corporation about the action toy that broke the day after Christmas.

Research, research and research

The students have already brainstormed some support for their positions. Now it's time for them to do any research they might need as supporting detail. They should find support to back up their opinions, which might include the following:

- Facts (e.g., *Second-hand smoke affects everyone, not just smokers.*)
- Statistics (e.g., *Forty-two percent of people who die of lung cancer have never smoked a cigarette.*)
- Statements from authorities (e.g., *Dr. T. O. Bacco, a lung specialist at the General Hospital, says that smoking in restaurants is the main source of second-hand smoke.*)
- General opinions (e.g., *All non-smokers agree that cigarettes and food don't mix.*)
- Reasoning (e.g., *If second-hand smoke can be bad for your health, imagine how much worse first-hand smoking must be.*)
- Examples or anecdotes (e.g., *Recently at the Brown Derby, only one table of smokers made dinner unpleasant for everyone.*)

Try to include as many examples and types of evidence as possible. Encourage students to search outside the Internet. It's far more impressive to cite a book or a serious magazine than an anonymous or company Web site. (See Chapter 6 for information about teaching students to do research.)

 MINI-LESSON: *Searching for Support*

Ask the students to use the topic they have chosen and search for outside support for their position. Challenge them to find

- one fact or statistic
- one "expert" statement or opinion
- one example or anecdote

Make sure that they provide the source for each piece of information they gather.

Plan the piece

Ask students to look at their ideas web or a list of supporting details and choose the three or four ideas they believe support their opinion most effectively. Have them rank ideas in order of strength.

Encourage your students to anticipate an argument against their position and to provide a rebuttal. They could include these ideas on an organizer.

We have provided two different persuasive writing organizers to help students organize their ideas and background information. (See pages 123 and 124.) Model both of them or decide which you would like the students to use as their planner. Then they will be ready to begin drafting.

Introduction
(usually one paragraph)

- Name the topic.
- Get the reader involved.
- State your opinion on the topic.
- Summarize your reasons.

Body
(one or more paragraphs)

- Give reasons for your opinion.
- Give facts and examples to support your opinion.
- Try to avoid using opinions to support opinions.

Conclusion
(one paragraph)

- Restate your opinion.
- Urge the reader to agree.
- End with a positive statement.

Drafting

Remember that the draft is an opportunity to get *all* ideas down on paper. Less effective details may be omitted later, but should not be lost at the outset.

As always, remind students to write their ideas as convincingly as possible, to write on only one side of the paper and to double-space their work. It is usually best to start by modeling some of your own writing before guiding the students through each step. Here is a series of steps for presenting procedural writing to your students.

State your opinion

Start with a strong statement or question that grabs the reader's attention and engages the reader in the text. Revisit "Six Great Ways to Start a Piece of Writing" on page 65 for reminders about effective leads. The introductory paragraph should identify the topic and state your opinion or thesis clearly. It should also include an overview of the reasons you plan to elaborate on to support your opinion.

Support your opinion

Think about the best order in which to present your evidence and support for your opinion. Keep your audience and purpose in mind as you write.

The body of the piece should consist of one paragraph for each idea with supporting details. You have already ranked your supporting ideas in order of strength. Here is one structure:

1. Your second strongest argument with support
2. Your least strong argument with support
3. The counterargument with your refuting statements
4. Your strongest argument last

Each argument should be backed up with one or more of the following:

- facts and statistics
- reasons
- examples and anecdotes
- descriptive detail
- quotes
- definitions

The size of the overall essay determines how many paragraphs a writer will want to use for the body. Young students may write only a single paragraph; junior high students should be able to write three to five body paragraphs.

Summarize your position to close

The conclusion should be brief and to the point. Close your argument with a strong statement that summarizes your position and what you would like the reader to do. A positive note at the end is always preferable to further outrage.

Revising

Revisit techniques of persuasive rhetoric outlined earlier in the chapter. Encourage students to use at least one in their persuasive writing.

Senior students should be able to anticipate arguments that might be used against their position. Addressing these arguments gives them a chance to head off the opposition as they put forward their own ideas.

The following chart is a good guide to effective persuasive writing. It is useful for teachers in providing feedback and advice, as well as for students in evaluating their own work and that of their peers. The persuasive writing checklist on page 125 is another effective revision tool.

What Effective Persuasive Writing Looks Like

Ideas	Organization	Voice	Word Choice	Sentence Fluency	Conventions
Thesis or opinion is clearly stated with lots of strong supporting detail, including facts, statistics, and other evidence.	Introduction engages the reader and states thesis clearly. Body is well organized. Conclusion reiterates and makes a strong positive statement.	Writer's passion for the issue is evident. Voice is engaging and appropriate to audience.	Word choice is powerful and passionate. Vocabulary is specific instead of vague.	Writing flows smoothly with balance of sentence types and lengths. Some Very Short Sentences are included.	Control over conventions of spelling, grammar and punctuation are appropriate to the level of the writer.

Editing and Publishing

It's worth reminding students that any argument they put forward publicly is seriously compromised by errors in spelling or grammar. Work that is to be published must be edited for spelling and conventions. Don't subject your students (and your teaching) to behind-the-back comments on quality simply because the final editing has been a bit careless.

One wonderful aspect of persuasive writing is that there are more venues for publishing finished works than for any other genre. Your students might want to

- participate in a debate
- present a piece as a speech
- post it on the school or class Web site
- send it to the local newspaper
- send it as a letter

In our 50 years of teaching (combined years – we're not *that* old), we've seen the fruits of classroom persuasive writing assignments appear in school newsletters, on Web sites, in local newspapers and in national magazines. With each instance of publication, our students' pride in their writing grows, and they learn of the power of the printed word. Be sure to share that power with your students.

No Smoking
by Nicole, Grade 4

I don't want people to smoke in restaurants, stores and other public places. There should be a Smoker's house, where smokers go and smoke all they want. This place can include a bar and TV and other sources that the people want. Each city would have a Smoker's house.

When smokers are in public, they could have a bubble, so the smoke won't come in the air. It can have a machine that doesn't let any of the smoke get in the air.

These are some inventions that I have made up. Now I will tell you why I don't want smokers at public places. I don't like smokers because when they smoke the people who are by them have to smell the smoke. When people smoke, the smoke can sometimes get into your body. The people who think smoking is cool, it's not, because it hurts you and other people too.

Should Gerbils Be Pets?
by Brandie, Grade 5

I'm going to talk about gerbils. Gerbils are small like mice, but more like hamsters. They aren't mean and don't bite a lot. Believe me, I had two. I love gerbils. They are cool.

Gerbils have many good qualities, like they are quiet. And they don't have many diseases. If you are in school, they are very convenient because they sleep during the day.

If you are thinking about a school pet, they are a lot like hamsters. If you are afraid they will run away, they won't if they have things to do and a sturdy cage. Everyone should love this pet. They are so cool, that's what I've found.

So, think about a gerbil! They are not very expensive, they fit in a cage and you don't have to let them outside or take them for a walk. You can take it out of the cage to play with and put it in a gerbil ball where it can run around your room. Buy a gerbil and have some fun.

Student Writing

I Hate Detentions!
by Chandy, Grade 6

I believe teachers shouldn't give detentions when kids are late! I have three good reasons why. First, sometimes teachers are late, and they just walk in like nothing happened and say, "Sorry I'm late." Then when we come in late, they say, "So when will I see you, at lunch?" or "Why are you so late?" That's not fair, and it's a double standard. Second, detentions are a huge waste of time. For example, if you are done everything and you get a detention for being late, you have to sit in an empty room for 15 minutes. Fifteen minutes doesn't sound like much. But it is if you're not doing anything. Third, my sister is really, really slow and my mom and dad make me wait for her, so she makes me late. Therefore, when I'm late because of her, it's really not my fault! For all of these reasons, I believe teachers should not give detentions because we are late.

Uniforms for Public Schools?
by Christine, Grade 8

What's the point? Why should kids wear uniforms? In school, you are taught to be creative and independent. How do uniforms enforce that? How do they enforce the rules?

Public schools are public. You don't have to be rich or famous to attend. If we have to wear uniforms, we might as well attend some private school in Sweden.

Uniforms rob your personality. I can remember many of my teachers saying that your personality will develop over the next few years. How can it develop when we all wear the same thing, every day, and never have any individuality? Everyone has different tastes, but they wouldn't be allowed to show or express them.

If you think uniforms will reduce teasing about the clothing kids wear, think again. If someone is set on teasing someone, they will say something along the lines of, "I look better in my uniform than you do." Therefore, we might as well wear normal clothing and get, "How come you wear that? Why not Tommy Hilfiger?" Those comments are easier to take.

I sincerely believe we shouldn't wear uniforms in school, simply because they don't make things better. And unless the teachers are prepared to wear a uniform, I'm certainly not!

Persuasive Writing Prompts for Student Writers

Below you can see a range of prompts appropriate for students at various levels.

Prompts for Students in Grades 1–2	Prompts for Students in Grades 3–6	Prompts for Students in Grades 7 and Up
• Should brothers and sisters have to share their toys?	• Is it safe to ride a bike without a helmet?	• Do brand names matter?
• Is it important to brush your teeth every day?	• Should parents always be in charge?	• Should teenagers be allowed to vote?
• What is your favorite season and why?	• Is it ever okay to lie?	• Should students be required to wear uniforms?
	• Is recess a good idea?	
• Who is your favorite person and why?	• If you found $10 on the floor of a store, would it be okay to keep the money?	• Should smoking be banned in public places?
• Is it okay to throw your garbage on the street?		• Should kids get paid for going to school?
	• Was the Big Bad Wolf really bad, or just misunderstood?	• Is skateboarding dangerous?
		• What time should school start in the morning?

Facts and Reasons Organizer

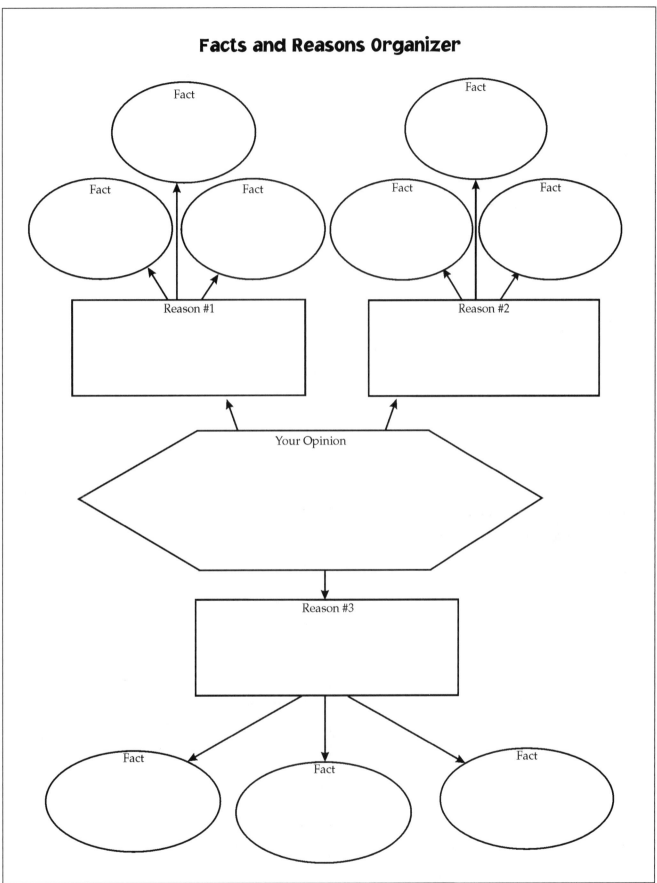

Persuasive Writing Organizer

Position or Opinion:

Strongest Reason ⟶	Support
Second Reason ⟶	Support
Third Reason ⟶	Support
Other people might argue . . .	But I say . . .

Persuasive Writing Checklist

Introduction: *Did you . . .*

- ❑ Start with a hook to grab the reader's interest?
- ❑ Identify the topic?
- ❑ State your opinion clearly?
- ❑ Give a brief summary of the main reasons for your opinion?

Body: *Did you . . .*

- ❑ Present your reasons in a logical order?
- ❑ Provide supporting details, facts and examples for each reason?
- ❑ Use one paragraph for each reason?
- ❑ Anticipate an argument on the reader's part and argue against it?
- ❑ Use at least one special persuasive writing technique?
- ❑ Avoid general words such as *"great," "nice," "awesome"*?
- ❑ Allow your voice and passion to show through?

Conclusion: *Did you . . .*

- ❑ Restate your opinion?
- ❑ End with a strong, positive statement?

What changes do you plan to make to improve your writing?

_____

_____

_____

_____

_____

_____

8

Doing It My Way – Procedural Writing

Procedural writing – or process writing – is everywhere we look: computer manuals, instructions to program your VCR, recipes, advice columns, technical writing, and even novels. Nora Ephron dropped recipes into her novel *Heartburn* in the 1980s. Paul dropped several sections of advice (written by one of the characters) into his latest young-adult novel, *Running the Bases*.

"Project Alan": Instruction Set 1

Alan, your immediate objective is to get a date. Your long-term objectives probably include kissing and making out, but stick to your immediate objective for now. Arrange for coffee tomorrow, then follow these instructions.

What to talk to Mel about:

1. *Her. No topic will be more fascinating to Melissa Halvorsen than herself. Admire her hair, her eyes, her brains, her charm, her wit. Girls love praise and admiration. Lay it on thick.*
2. *Her interests. Find out something about ringette. Talk about it. I hear she watches her brother's football games, ask her about them.*
3. *Her concerns, thoughts, etc. Since she's only 15, it's likely that Mel doesn't have many thoughts . . . but admire whatever she puts forward.*

Alan, you'll notice that there's no room in the list above for YOUR interests. Therefore, do not talk about video games, your favorite TV shows, your problems in school, or your jerky friends. Nobody cares.

As you can see, procedural writing is not only practical, but fun to do. It lends itself to exercises in clear thought and communication, opportunities to practise many different forms of writing, and even tongue-in-cheek humor. Moreover, procedural writing is one of the few genres where graphic design and illustrations are important elements of communication. Your young artists will have a chance to use their skills.

Reading "How-to" Texts

Although your students are reading procedural text all the time, they probably don't even realize its unique elements. Prepare a collection of text samples to bring into class: the manual for your new DVD player, a couple of recipes, directions to your school from a MapQuest Web site, the rules for playing a game, a page from a craft book, step-by- step instructions for assembling a bookshelf or an excerpt from a travel guide. Look for procedural writing in a variety of different formats: complete sentences and paragraphs as well as numbered steps. Shel Silverstein's poem "My Rules" would be an entertaining addition to the collection. ("If you want to marry me, here's what you have to do . . . ")

With the students, talk about what these texts have in common and what the differences are. (You may want to create a chart or Venn diagram to outline these elements.) From the discussion, work together to create a framework for procedural writing. It should look something like this:

PROCEDURAL WRITING FRAMEWORK

Purpose	Organization
To tell how to do something	BEGINNING: Tells what the purpose of the procedure is MIDDLE: Outlines materials that will be needed and steps to follow END: Reviews what the end result should be
	Language Features
	❊ Factual language and tone ❊ No extraneous description or detail ❊ Technical vocabulary ❊ Second-person voice ❊ Imperative sentences, usually with the subject (you) implicit ❊ Transitions that define chronology: *first, next, after that*
	Examples
	Manuals, directions, recipes, instructions, rules

Here's a homework assignment for your students: Have them bring a piece of procedural writing from home to display on the bulletin board. You may even want to issue a challenge to try to find a kind of procedure that no one else will bring.

In addition to the student samples, there are many books for children and adults that would be useful for teaching both reading *and* writing of procedural text:

- craft and cook books
- *Life's Little Instruction Book*
- any of the "For Dummies" books
- Web sites: From MapQuest to How to Play Lacrosse
- sports and games books
- some of the "Worst Case Scenarios" books

Obviously, when using adult materials, you will want to be selective about reading choices for your students. We strongly discourage putting out books that you haven't screened carefully first.

Give your students plenty of opportunity to read these different types of procedural texts and to note the common characteristics and unique features before starting to write.

 MINI-LESSON: *Looking for Graphics Features*

Most kids are already familiar with clip art from their work with computers and word processing. That's why their cover pages sometimes get more effort than the body of the text. In procedural writing, designers use many elements – from type choice to bullets to illustrations to boxed text – all designed to make the text more "friendly" and useful to the readers.

As they read, ask your students to list ten visual or graphics features they notice in procedural writing. In addition to noting or sketching each feature, have them explain why it was chosen by the designer and how it helps (or impedes) the reading.

Compare the lists. When you're finished, the kids should have an enlarged repertoire of graphics features and their purposes that they will be able to use in their own work.

Graphics in Procedural Text:

- numbered lists
- bulleted lists
- titles and heads
- subheads
- italicized and bold type
- columns
- text boxes
- shaded boxes
- different typefaces
- drawings
- pictures
- diagrams
- cartoons
- logos
- sidebar information
- footnotes

The Challenge of Clear Directions

Now the fun begins. Your students know about different kinds of procedural texts and how they're structured. But they probably don't realize just how challenging it is to write clear and specific directions. Here's a demonstration to make that point.

MINI-LESSON: *The Baloney Sandwich Procedure*

You will need

- a loaf of bread
- a package of sliced baloney
- a jar of mustard
- a knife for spreading
- a plate

Your students are going to give you the directions for making a baloney sandwich. Tell them that you will do exactly what they tell you to do. They can take turns giving one instruction at a time.

You may end up with mustard on your desk, on your fingers or on your nose. These are the risks of dynamic teaching.

Do *exactly* what they say, as if you were from Mars and had never even seen a slice of baloney ever before. If a student tells you to put the baloney on the bread, then place the whole package of baloney on top of the loaf of bread. If someone tells you to get mustard on the knife before taking the lid off the jar, make a big show of trying to stick the knife through the lid. If the instruction is unclear, say, "I don't understand that instruction" or interpret it in some silly way. Note: Allow time for laughter.

The kids will soon find that their instructions are out of sequence or unclear or even contradictory. You may end up with mustard on your desk, on your fingers or on your nose. These are the risks of dynamic teaching. In our experience, it will take more than 25 instructions for your class to tell you how to make the sandwich.

Be sure to talk with the students about what they can learn from this experience. For example, directions must be stated clearly and in the correct order. The procedural writer must know who the audience is and how much background knowledge they have. Obviously, instructions must be planned carefully to avoid baloney and mustard disaster.

You may want to follow up by having students write out the directions for making a baloney sandwich. The next day, put students in groups to test one another's directions. Keep wet paper towels on hand for any messy results!

 MINI-LESSON: *Follow My Instructions*

Reproduce the pictures in "Follow My Instructions" on page 139 or use others of your choice. Divide the students into pairs. Only one person gets to see the picture and he must tell his partner how to draw it. His job is to provide step-by-step *oral* directions for his partner. The partner gets only a blank sheet of paper and cannot see the picture until after he is done drawing. Then switch, using a different picture. This activity will give the students practice in providing explicit instructions to achieve a goal.

After both students have had a chance to compare their drawings to the original picture, have them talk about their success and what they might have done to give better directions.

In no other kind of writing is it so important for writers to know for whom they are writing. As students will learn from the sandwich-making experience, the teacher from outer space who has never made a sandwich before needs clear, explicit directions. On the other hand, someone writing a computer repair manual for an experienced technician can assume she has certain background knowledge and technical vocabulary. The audience makes a difference.

Revisiting the RAFTS format is a good idea at this point. The students will be writing in the role of an expert on a specific topic. The strong verb will be to *teach* someone *how* to do something. The writer will have to decide on a topic and the format that goes with it. However, the audience will be the biggest influence on how the text will be created.

Writers of procedural texts should consider these questions: Are you writing for someone who already has thorough background knowledge in this topic? Do you need to explain technical vocabulary? Do you need to proceed in very small steps or can you assume that gaps will be filled in by the reader's background knowledge? For example, a recipe direction to "reduce" the sauce would be clear to a cook, but useless to a garage mechanic.

Unfortunately, not all manuals pay attention to their audience. Our home is filled with manuals for appliances and home entertainment systems that baffle us, in spite of our passable intelligence and many years of schooling. Part of the problem is that many of our electronics are produced in Asia, with the directions translated quite literally into English and other languages. Directions for use of our favorite rice cooker, for example, tell us, "Never use force in washing the kettle as this may cause dents on it, resulting to insufficient cooking."

Pre-writing

A good starting point is to have the students make a top ten list of things they are good at.

The best place to start with procedural writing comes from the students' own experience: how to brush your teeth, how to put on lipstick, how to kick a soccer ball. Sometimes these activities are so automatic that kids don't even think about all the stages involved. That's why asking them to practise the step-by-step logic needed for procedural writing makes a good warm-up exercise. Start by having the students make a top ten list of things they are good at. These may range from playing the drums to setting the table to bugging an older sister to getting out of setting the table. Their lists will give them a repertoire of topics for exploring the procedural genre.

Later, you'll get more interesting writing – and the students will learn more – if they are required to pick a topic that requires a little research; How to Become a Pilot and How to Survive an Avalanche are good examples.

Another good motivational approach, which Paul has used with high-school students, is to have the class brainstorm a large topic for which *everyone* will write a small section. Topics such as Ways to Improve Our School, Advice to Parents and How to Survive Grade 8 can be broken down into many different features and columns.

The next decision to make is what type of format will suit the topic that has been chosen. Some procedures, like recipes, are little more than lists. Others are written in paragraph form, either in narrative or expository style. But most are a combination of both. For example, Lori is reluctantly reading a weight-loss guide that outlines a series of explicit procedures ("seven simple steps to change your life overnight") with several paragraphs of explanation, description and research for each. You will want your students to write at least one procedure in a format that combines research, personal knowledge and writer's craft, within the structure of the procedural genre.

You may be surprised how receptive community members are to helping students with projects, if they are polite and well prepared. Lori once had her Grade 4 students interview local celebrities, from the premier of the province to the professional football coach, for their classroom newspaper.

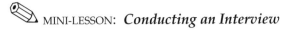 MINI-LESSON: *Conducting an Interview*

We talked about techniques for gathering research in Chapter 6. But some of the best material for an article or procedural piece will come from speaking with an expert. An expert can offer your student writers solid facts, colorful background information and some interesting quotes to spice up their text.

Students need to know a few basics before they go out to do an interview:

- Time is valuable for professionals. The interview should last no longer than 20 minutes.
- When calling or visiting to ask for an appointment, students must be clear about the purpose for the interview: "I'm writing an article about how an expert decorates a cake. Could I speak to you some time this week for about 20 minutes?" This approach gets the attention of the expert and will usually be enough to get an interview time.
- Students must show up for the interview ten minutes ahead of time. Late interviewers get short-shrift responses.
- Make *absolutely* sure that your students are well prepared. They should have 5 to 10 good questions prepared in advance. Teach them to avoid "yes or no" questions or to follow them up with "why?"
- The best interviews go beyond the prepared questions. One answer may lead to another good question that might not have been on the list. Encourage students to think on their feet and to invite the expert to say more.
- Remind students to bring a tape recorder, but also to take notes. Tape recorders have been known to fail just when interviewers need them most.
- Telephone interviews are also an option, but face-to-face is always better.

Probably many of your students will be nervous about interviewing a "real" adult. You can help them overcome the feeling by providing opportunities for partnership and practice. For partnership, send the kids out in twos to do the interview. One partner can ask questions; the other can hold a tape recorder in his trembling hands. As far as practice goes, have students practise each stage of the interview, from phoning the expert to introducing themselves to asking the questions and offering thanks. The students can role-play in pairs, asking real questions. Then, arm them with tape recorders and send them out into the real world.

Ultimately, your students will need a set of notes, Internet page print-offs, copies of articles from books and magazines, and whatever else they can find that will help them write the procedural essay. If the assignment is a research-based procedure, part of their mark – we recommend 20 percent in this genre – should be for the collected research materials.

Drafting

During drafting, the students should also be thinking about what kinds of graphics to use and when to use them. But the text should come first. The basic sentence structure for procedural writing is the imperative sentence, or command. Although this type of sentence will be very familiar to your students, you may want to do a quick mini-lesson on its grammatical structure.

 MINI-LESSON: *Sentence Sorting*

Sentence sorts are a great way to teach and reinforce many different language concepts. Provide your students with several sentences and have them sort them according to sentence type. You may even tell them to sort them into commands (imperative sentences) and statements (declarative sentences). Here are some sample sentences for sorting:

- *Please take out your books and begin to read.*
- *All of the students were concentrating on their assignments.*
- *Don't break that vase!*
- *Insert the strap into the buckle and pull tightly.*
- *He washed the windows after he dusted the furniture.*

After sorting, the students must come up with a generalization to define each type of sentence. Guide your students to identify the key characteristics of an imperative sentence: the understood "you" as the subject and the action verb that drives the predicate. This process of categorizing and generalizing will help your students internalize and transfer their understanding of the sentence type that forms the foundation of procedural writing.

 MINI-LESSON: *The Imperative Sentence Game*

Play the imperative sentence game. Choose a procedural theme, such as how to get rich quick or how to lose a friend. Using a set of verb cards, such as those on page 140, have students take turns drawing a card and coming up with an imperative sentence beginning with that verb.

 MINI-LESSON: *Sentence Strip Writing*

Bonus! You can teach your students to plan and draft at the same time using sentence strips. This lesson teaches drafting, revision and organization all in one.

Cut some paper into strips, each a few centimetres wide, and provide each student with a set of about a dozen strips. Model or guide the students through a common task – perhaps starting a car – then allow the students to work on their own topics. Each step of the procedure should be written on a separate strip of paper. The writers can then physically manipulate their sentence strips to place them in the correct

Have the students work in pairs the first time they do this activity. The discussions they have as they plan, draft and revise will be as instructive as the activity itself.

order and identify gaps and redundancies. They can also use scissors and tape to separate or combine ideas as needed.

When the students are satisfied that they have all the steps in place, in clear and logical order, they can glue them onto larger sheets, word-process them or copy them out by hand.

Revising

The usual revision routines will work as well for procedural writing as any other genre. TAG conferences with a student peer will often reveal some gaps and flaws in the writing, but perhaps not enough to lead to an effective procedure. If possible, your students should be encouraged or required to do what professional technical and recipe writers do: test it out.

A recipe doesn't make it into a cookbook until someone has followed the instructions to prepare the dish. A set of instructions that looks wonderfully clear to the author and editor may be missing key steps or ingredients. "How come I need jalapenos in step five when they're not in the ingredient list?" asks the tester. "We'll fix it," replies the author/editor. The proof of a recipe's success, one might say, is in the pudding.

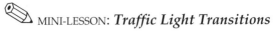 MINI-LESSON: *Traffic Light Transitions*

Many students have trouble making smooth transitions from one idea to another, but transitions are easy to teach. To teach transition words that depict chronological order, you can make an analogy to traffic lights.

- *Green* light words tell the reader to get started. These are words like "first," "to start with" and "at the beginning."
- *Yellow* light words tell the reader to continue on. Words like "next," "after that" and "then" remind the reader to keep reading.
- *Red*, of course, means stop. Red light words tell the reader that the text is ending. Words include "at last," "finally," and "in the end."

Make three charts, each with an appropriate traffic light symbol. Together with your students, generate a list of words for each. Display the charts as an ongoing reference and continue adding to them as the year goes on.

Have students go back into their drafts to ensure that they have included appropriate transition words for clarity and effect.

The following chart is a guideline for assessing student procedural writing and can provide ideas for improvement.

What Effective Procedural Writing Looks Like

Ideas	Organization	Voice	Word Choice	Sentence Fluency	Conventions
The author presents ideas in a complete, coherent way, without extraneous or missing detail.	Ideas and descriptions are presented in a logical sequence; instructions are in chronological sequence.	Writing reflects an authoritative tone and style, appropriate to genre, purpose and audience.	The author chooses effective, specific verbs; transition words support sequence.	Clarity is most important. There may not be as much rhythm and variety as in other genres.	Capitalization and punctuation seem effective and logical; words are spelled appropriately for the writer's developmental level.

Editing and Publishing

As always, remind students to apply the CUPS strategy for editing (see page 24) to ensure that all of the conventions are correct before publishing. Then, have your students do a second run-through to attend to the visual elements of the text. Magazines have separate editors for text and for visual images. Your students should learn to look at these elements separately, too.

- Is this picture in the right spot?
- Does this graphic need to be so big?
- Is the font the right size and in the right place?
- Does this illustration show what it's supposed to show?
- Should this list of bulleted points be numbered or not?
- Is the whole piece too long, too short, or just right?

Once your students have attended to surface edits, they are ready to publish. Procedural text is among the most publishable forms of writing. Your kids can become acclaimed authors and you a brilliant teacher with just a little attention to form and style.

Formats for published procedures may range from bound classroom anthologies to three-fold brochures. It may be the time to offer a mini-lesson on your school's desktop publishing program. Show students how they can find clip art and insert it into their text. If your students do not have access to a computer, or they're too young to word-process the information, old-fashioned cut and paste will work. Appropriate illustrations can be photocopied, trimmed with scissors and pasted into the article at the appropriate point.

Some students, of course, will want to create their own graphics. Before they begin to draw, however, they need to have a clear idea of what should be shown in each illustration. Have them sketch a layout of what they want the page to look like. Professional illustrators use their own version of the writing process for these illustrations: (1) making a plan for what is to be drawn, (2) making decisions on form, size and shape (3) doing a rough sketch, (4) creating a finished drawing, and (5) making revisions or redrawing entirely after conversation with editor and art director. It's not enough for your kids to say, "Oh, I know what I want to draw." Your answer should be, "Show me the plan."

School photocopiers work wonders in producing small booklets for a local audience. A nominal charge, say 25 cents, keeps copies from being wasted and provides a small sum of money for school or class benefit.

Reading procedural text is probably the most common type of reading people do in the everyday world. From programming the DVD player to assembling the new computer desk to driving to an unfamiliar location, we are constantly dealing with procedural texts. Learning how to write procedures is also important for students. It teaches them to be clear, concise and specific. It encourages the planning and creation of print pieces that are understandable and visually appealing. Perhaps in procedural text, more than in any other genre, learning to write well provides students with a skill set they will need for literacy beyond the classroom.

Recipe for a Thankful Thanksgiving

by Matthew, Grade 4

1 1/2 cups of patience
a dash of kindness
2 squirts of caring words
2 tbsp. of personality
a pinch of cooperation
4 tsp. of hospitality
1/4 cup of generosity
1 3/4 cups of love

First, you mix in the love, personality, patience, cooperation, and generosity. Then you stir in the kindness, caring words, and hospitality. When you finish that, you bake at a really, really high level. Then, when it's finished, you sprinkle it on everyone's plate.

The Right Way to Make Bat Wing Stew

by Allyson, Grade 5

The right way to make bat wing stew (as every good witch should know) is to start out in front of a blazing fire with a box of snake flakes, a large cauldron, and a magic book. The right magic book should be *Merlin's Guide to Witch Craft* or *Five Thousand Years Under a Spell*.

With your snake flakes at your side, put 3 1/2 cups of the flakes into a large jar. Shake for 2 minutes and let the snake flakes rest (in peace) for 300 years.

Add 4 cups of frog warts, then stir lightly. Pour the mixture into the cauldron.

Add 6 cups of "little-boy-pie-mix" along with 3/4 cups of eyeballs.

Now, add some Jetson rockets to give the stew a blast! Make sure you squish and stir well.

Add 2 1/2 cups of burned-to-the-crisp human hair. Now let the whole mixture bubble for 125 years. Then squish and stir again. Let it sit for 10 years before finally adding the stale bat wings. Then, chow down!

To order more copies of this wonderful stomach-wrenching stew, write to 277 Ghoulwood or fax 1-833-476-1844.

Student Writing

How to Entertain a Crowd with a Puppet

by Lauren, Grade 6

Puppet: a small cloth object that resembles a person, animal, household object and even the seasons. For entertainment, education and self-help uses. Operated by expert puppeteers.

Puppets are usually made to represent something, but on the same subject there are many different kinds of puppets, the easiest to operate being the hand puppet. Hand puppets are usually seen on a small stage high off the ground, making room for people to hide behind it, which makes being a puppeteer a breeze! Now this particular kind of puppet has a large hole at the bottom and usually a face at the top. Inside are little pockets to put your fingers in to work the puppet. The best of the best puppets are usually colourful and look very realistic.

To work this darling fabric pastime, simply slide your favourite hand into the large hole at the bottom and put your fingers in the pockets I was telling you about just now. If you are having some troubles trying to fit your fingers into the pockets, your pinkie and ring finger go in the far left, your middle and pointer finger go in the one straight ahead, next your thumb in the right pocket and then move your hand! Now you're all set!

Puppets are loads of fun and you made the right choice learning how they work. Soon people like Sesame Street and Mr. Dressup will be hiring you to work their famous puppets. You now know everything that I know about hand puppets. If you're really good, you'll learn and maybe even study about the puppets in Japan.

How to Clean Your Bedroom
by Amanda, Grade 8

The first step to cleaning up your room is picking your clothes off of the floor. They do not like to be wadded into a ball and left in a heap. Put them in a closet, a dresser, or a laundry hamper. Laundry hampers need to be fed every day.

The next step is to clean your dresser. Dressers do not want to be piled with junk. Junk is evil! Do not hoard it, hate it! Junk doesn't have arms or legs, so it cannot get to a garbage can. Help is on its way. Dressers don't like to be rammed with a vacuum cleaner or doused with cheap perfume until their varnish peels. Try to avoid these things.

The word "closet" means a small cabinet, compartment or room for storage. Do not confuse this with "storage shed." A closet can only hold so many items. Do not house anything in it that is going to need eight hours of sunlight or it will snarl at your mother when she opens the door.

Carpeting likes to be seen. It longs for attention. It is happy when people walk on it and say, "What lovely carpeting you have!" Carpeting doesn't like to be covered with clothes or paper. If something is lying on the carpeting, pick or vacuum it up.

Sleeping on a bed is an act of civility. Civilized people make their beds every day. They do not use them as a place to store books or clothes. Animals do this. Animals sleep outside. Observe this rule and you will never have to sleep outside.

Student Writing

Follow My Instructions

These pictures may be cut apart and distributed to pairs of students. One student instructs the other in how to draw the picture while the other, without seeing the picture, must draw it according to the instructions.

The Imperative Sentence Game

Directions: Cut apart the verb cards and put them in a can. As the can is passed around, each student draws a card and must come up with an imperative sentence beginning with the verb on that card. Choose a theme for all of the sentences to follow. Here are some ideas:

- How to Get Rich Quickly
- How to Drive Your Sister Crazy
- How Make Friends
- How to Lose Friends

- How to Impress Your Teacher
- How to Cook a Great Meal
- How to Get on a Team
- How to Win a Talent Contest

Stop	Change	Practise	Follow
Watch	Make	Write	Separate
Open	Close	Call	Get
Answer	Mix	Bake	Save
Spend	Give	Stir	Pay

9

More Than Rhyme Time – Poetry

Debates about the virtues of poetry and prose go back to the sixteenth century in English literature. Poetry has a certain elegance and style, which is why we so often reserve it for special occasions and elevated emotions. Shakespeare saved his verse for noble characters and left prose to poor Bottom and his crew of rude servants; Molière made jokes about the same class distinctions. But prose has been fighting its way up the social ladder for centuries, and today the differences in use are often blurred.

Poetry holds a natural appeal for children from the youngest ages to those of us who just think we're young. That's why we recite nursery rhymes and read Dr. Seuss to our pre-schoolers. Readers of all ages generally associate poetry with rhyme; in fact, many of us don't realize that there is any other kind of poetry. As a result, we often get student poetry that reads like this:

> The cat
> Sat on the mat
> And got fat.

For young poets, the effort to rhyme often supersedes meaning and voice. These students need to learn that poetry, like prose, is intended to present an idea; rhyme is only one tool to help convey that meaning. For this reason, we recommend that you avoid asking students to write rhyming poetry until they have had many opportunities to write free (unrhymed) verse.

All too often in middle school, our poetry units seem to follow the "If it's Tuesday, it must be haiku" format. In an effort to broaden students' experiences with other forms of poetry, we sometimes limit them to rigid structures, such as haiku or cinquain. While these are legitimate literacy activities that serve specific purposes, they are not a complete poetry program. What we need to do is expose students to a range of poetic forms and styles so that they understand the unique characteristics of poetry and use it to express their ideas in a way that is not possible with prose.

Surprisingly, poetry is often an appealing genre for reluctant readers. Because it is usually short, they think it's going to be easy. As a result, they're more willing to take risks about reading and writing poetry. Although poetry is never as easy as it looks, we can take advantage of this interest to provide the students with a set of tools for writing poetry, then send them off to experiment with the structures and elements that enable them to convey their ideas most effectively.

Marinate Students in the Genre

Don't merely immerse your students in poetry; *marinate* them in it. (Allow us some poetic licence here.) Bring a collection of published anthologies into your classroom and provide students with plenty of school time to read them. There are many different styles and forms of poetry, and we want our students to have a sense of the diversity before they begin to write.

Remember that much poetry is meant to be read aloud. Be sure to provide many opportunities for students to engage in individual, shared and performance reading of poetry. They can practise oral reading fluency, phrasing and expression. Have the students choose favorite poems to interpret and read to the class – and be sure to share some "teacher's choices" as well.

Divide students into groups of three or four and assign each group a poem of one page or less to prepare and present to the class. (Many of the poems of Shel Silverstein or Dennis Lee are appropriate and appealing.) The students in the group must work together to decide who will say which lines and what they will say in unison. They have to attend to rhythms and pauses, and practise volume, tempo, tone and expression.

While continuing to read poetry, introduce brief writing exercises that enable students to sharpen the tools of poetry writing: rhythm, shape, musical language, repetition, sensory imagery and rhyme. Not only will these activities create a toolbox of techniques, but the guided writing will build your students' confidence in their ability to write poetry. Then your fledgling poets can be set free to write their own poems.

 MINI-LESSON: *The Difference Between Poetry and Prose*

What is the difference between a poem and a story? If you ask your students the answer to this question, they are likely to come up with two ideas: poetry rhymes and poetry is shorter. You need to provide them with a clearer perspective.

Show the students some short examples of well-crafted descriptive prose. Some examples can be found in the following picture books:

Owl Moon by Jane Yolen
Twilight Comes Twice by Ralph Fletcher
The Other Way to Listen by Byrd Baylor
Dogteam by Gary Paulsen

Then show the students some free verse (unrhymed) poetry. You will find examples in the works of many modern poets for children, including Eve Merriam, George Swede, Charlotte Zolotow, Langston Hughes and Carl Sandburg.

Use a chart to outline the features that distinguish poetry from prose. Your list will probably include these points:

- a unique treatment of an ordinary topic
- poetic use of descriptive language
- precise and economical word choice
- focus on the sounds of language as well as the meaning
- repetition of sounds, words and phrases for effect
- attention to line breaks and "white space"
- sometimes a formal structure (sonnet, ballad, etc.)

Teaching the "Tools" of Poetry

A poet uses many "tools" to shape language to suit an idea and a purpose. Here are some examples:

- rhythm
- musical language
- sensory imagery
- comparisons
- shape and form
- rhyme

These poetic devices are discussed in more detail on the following pages.

Rhythm

One characteristic that distinguishes poetry from prose is the rhythm and cadence of the language. Some poetry has a strong beat, while much free verse has a subtle or irregular rhythm. It's very important to expose students to a variety of poetic forms, so they learn to listen for many types of rhythms.

Repetition of sounds, words and ideas adds to the power and precision of poetry. (Now there's alliteration!) Sometimes the first line of the poem is repeated at the end. Sometimes a word or phrase is repeated internally to enhance the rhythm. Go on a scavenger hunt for effective use of repetition in poetry. Invite students to share the words and passages they chose and talk about how the repetition enhanced the meaning and sound of the poem.

Students sometimes understand this idea better if you make analogies to music. Have them tap different rhythms as they listen to music, then do the same thing as they listen to poetry or read it aloud. Those wonderful archaic terms – *iamb*, *trochee*, *spondee*, *anapest* – come from musical rhythms that existed long before they were applied by the Greeks to poetry.

Musical language

Effective word choice is one of the strongest elements of good poetry. Because poetry is characterized by economical use of language, every

Let's leave the limericks in Ireland! By middle school, your students have written enough limericks and anagram poems to last them a lifetime. It's time for some other poetry – rhymed or free verse.

word must be deliberately and carefully chosen for its meaning, sound and relationship to the other words in the poem.

Think about the order of the words. Some word patterns are simply more rhythmical than others. There's a reason we say "peaches and cream" instead of "cream and peaches." Encourage students to listen for the music of language in their writing and to experiment with the order of words and phrases. Some literary devices that contribute to rhythm and cadence are outlined below.

- **Onomatopoeia** is a wonderful term that means words that sound like the actions or sounds they represent, such as "bang," "rrriippp," or "buzz."

  Together with the students, write some "onomatopoetry." Make noises such as crumpling a piece of paper or scraping shoes against the floor. Have students brainstorm descriptive words that represent those sounds. Work together to put the words into a poem.

- **Invented words** sometimes convey a message more effectively than real ones. For younger students, Jon Scieszka's *Baloney, Henry P.* is full of wonderful words that sound made up, but are actually real words from other languages. Older students will enjoy reading Lewis Carroll's "Jabberwocky" and discussing his word choices. Have students take chunks of text and rewrite with their own made-up words.

- **Alliteration** refers to a pattern in which two or more words begin with the same sound. Alliteration was the basis of our earliest poetry in the English language and remains particularly important in languages where rhyming is either too easy or too difficult. Alliterative patterns contribute to the rhythm and cadence of the language.

  Look for examples of alliteration in published poetry and share them with the class. Traditional poets such as Tennyson and Walter de la Mare offer good examples, as do many contemporary poets such as Toni Morrison.

 MINI-LESSON: *Alliterative Poems*

Alliterative poems enable students to play with words and sounds without worrying too much about meaning. Assign each student a letter of the alphabet – perhaps the first letter of their own names. Encourage them to enlist the aid of a dictionary to generate interesting-sounding words that begin with that letter. They can then put the words together in a way that is rhythmical – and syntactically correct – if not particularly logical.

- **Vigorous verbs** are a key source of energy in powerful writing of any kind; poetry is no exception. Students could use *Hoops*, a book about basketball by Robert Burleigh, as a model to create sound and verb poems based on action-packed pictures from sports magazines.

Go on a word hunt for strong verbs in poetry. Jack Prelutsky's "The Turkey Shot out of the Oven" is a great example.

 MINI-LESSON: *Verb Poems*

Create poems out of "ing" verbs! Weather-related topics, such as snow, rain, wind or lightning, work well. Brainstorm "ing" verbs related to the topic, such as *pouring, drizzling, pelting*. Write each word on a card. Together, experiment with putting the verbs together into a poem. Think about which ones sound good together and convey the meaning most effectively. Delete words that don't work and feel free to add other words, like prepositional phrases. After you have worked through this as a group, have students write their own verb poems.

Sensory imagery

Effective poetry evokes sights, sounds, textures and even smells and tastes. Read this excerpt from Matthew Arnold's "Dover Beach":

> *Only, from the long line of spray*
> *Where the sea meets the moon-blanched land,*
> *Listen! you hear the grating roar*
> *Of pebbles which the waves draw back, and fling,*
> *At their return, up the high strand,*
> *Begin, and cease, and then again begin.*

Try to imagine this poem without the visual image of the beach and the sound of the waves. You can begin to see how sensory imagery brings the poetry to life. It is for sense, music and language that we read poetry – and these are the qualities we are trying to encourage when our students write.

Read a piece of poetry aloud and have students sketch what they envision as they listen. Then pass out photographs of landscapes (post-cards work well) and ask the children to write about the images they evoke. They can later turn their ideas into poems.

Comparisons

Poets use similes and metaphors to create images by making unusual comparisons that lead us to see things in new, fresh ways. Similes are easier for kids: "He was as happy as a pig a-snortin' and a-wallowin' in that there mud"; metaphors require a greater imaginative stretch: "The moon was a ghostly galleon tossed upon cloudy seas." Both modes of comparison will enrich your students' language in poetry and in the rest of their writing.

Judi Barrett's picture book *Things That Are Most in the World* describes the quietest, strongest, wiggliest and softest things in the world. You can use her book as a springboard for your class creating "Most in the World" poems. Nancy Lee Cecil offers this framework in *For the Love of Language*:

The oldest (smallest, loudest . . .) thing in the world is _____
It is (color) like _____
It is _____
And smells (tastes, looks, feels) like _____

MINI-LESSON: *Fun Food Writing*

Give each student a treat such as an Oreo cookie or a handful of Smarties. Brainstorm ways to describe how the treat looks and smells. Have students take one bite and describe how it sounds, tastes and feels in the mouth. Together, complete the chart below, using words that are as descriptive as possible. Then let the students work individually or in groups to put these ideas into a poem.

Looks Like	Smells Like	Sounds Like	Feels Like	Tastes Like

 MINI-LESSON: *Color Carousel*

Hailstones and Halibut Bones by Mary O'Neill is a wonderful book of poems about colors. Read four or five of the poems aloud to your students and record the color images on separate charts. Post the charts around the room and have students travel in groups of three or four to each chart, brainstorming their own ideas about that color. Every two minutes tell the groups to move to the next station on the circle, or carousel. Remind the students to use all their senses, not just the visual. What does blue taste like? What does red sound like? After each group has visited all of the charts on the circle, there will be a large collection of vocabulary related to each of the colors. Now the students will be ready to create color poems of their own, using some of the words on the charts and adding others of their own. A student might choose to write an entire poem on one color or a rainbow poem with one or two lines for each color.

Shape and form

The white space between (or included in) the line of poetry can be almost as important as the text. Just as a musical composer must choose where to place his rests, so a poet determines where to break lines in order to create the most effective rhythm and sound. Poetry can take many different forms according to the impression the poet wishes to make. Teaching shape and form is an appropriate opportunity to introduce formal structures such as diamante and haiku.

 MINI-LESSON: *Diamante Poetry*

Paul: I thought we just said we should abandon pattern poems.

Lori: They shouldn't be our whole poetry program, but sometimes we can use them for a specific purpose – like demonstrating shape and form with diamante, or practising precise word choice with haiku.

Although we caution against overuse of patterns and frameworks, there are times that teaching a pattern can help students learn about specific elements such as shape, form, and economical use of language. Diamante is a parallel-structure poetry format in a diamond shape: the top and bottom of the diamond are single nouns, the opposite of each other, such as "day" and "night." The second line consists of two adjectives describing the noun in the first line. The fourth line consists of two adjectives describing the noun in the last line. The middle line consists of four "ing" verbs or gerunds, two describing the first noun and two describing the last noun. Here's an example you might use with your students.

Winter
Frosty, Frozen
Snowing, Blowing, Flowering, Growing
Sunny, Breezy
Summer

Rhyme

Okay, here it is . . . at last. We've deliberately left rhyme till the end to show students that there's much more to poetry than rhyming text. Nonetheless, rhyming poetry has great appeal for many readers and some students become very skillful at writing rhymes. The thing to remember is not to sacrifice meaning and rhythm for the sake of rhymes. Emphasize that good rhyming poetry generally has a strong rhythm as well.

Reference books such as rhyming dictionaries are useful to help students generate rhyming text that has rhythm and cadence. They also remove some of the mental grunt work required to come up with a rhyme. We suggest that students start with rhyming couplets before tackling more complex rhyme patterns such as *ABAB* or limericks.

The Writing Process in Poetry

By now, your students should have a toolbox full of poetry techniques and a folder full of poetry exercises that may be turned into polished and published poetry. (There we go again with the alliteration!)

Pre-writing

Brainstorm topics that students are interested in. Although many adult poems are about love and romance, these topics aren't likely to motivate your students. Urge them to think about subjects related to everyday life: sports, school, friends and enemies. Bear in mind that some of the most interesting poems treat ordinary subjects in a unique way. (Witness Shel Silverstein's tribute to the toilet plunger.)

If you have students who struggle to get started, they may want to use some models from familiar poems as springboards. Here are a few suggestions from Silverstein.

- "Hector the Collector" – What other things could Hector collect?
- "If the World Was Crazy" – What if the *school* was crazy?
- "Recipe for a Hippopotamus Sandwich" – A _____ sandwich is easy to make . . .
- "For Sale" – Create a convincing ad to sell your brother or sister.
- "Who" – Exaggerate about what you can or would like to do.

Drafting

Some writers like to brainstorm a few ideas before they begin writing; others brainstorm as they draft. The advantage of poetry is its brevity – students can move ideas around with ease. Drafting/brainstorming lines of poetry on individual strips of paper makes it easy to manipulate the shape and flow later.

"What if . . . " poems by Shel Silverstein, John Ciardi and Ogden Nash are good samples to use for this lesson.

 MINI-LESSON: *Sentence Strip Poetry*

For this lesson, students choose a topic that lends itself to a list format. Ask them to compose each line of poetry on a separate strip of paper. After they have generated all their ideas, have them choose the best ones and move the strips of paper around to get the most meaningful and interesting sequence, as well as the most rhythmical sound. The writers can then cut up the strips of paper (or tape them together) to plan effective line breaks, and add or delete material as needed. After editing for conventions, they can recopy the poem or glue the strips onto another sheet of paper in their final form.

Revising

Many published poets rework their poetry 50 to 100 times (e.e. cummings was very proud of this). Students who think poetry springs full-blown from the heart, perfect in every way, simply don't understand how real poets work or how real poetry gets written. In order to craft poetry, writers have to work at it – often much more assiduously than they'd work at revising prose.

To model revision, choose a published poem – or use one of your own – and read it aloud three times. The first time, ask yourself, "Does it all make sense?" On the second reading, ask, "Did I use the right words to create mental pictures and evoke appropriate feelings?" And on the third reading, ask, "Does the poem sound musical and rhythmical?" Then have students do the same with their own poems. This process should provide ideas for revising the poem.

When conferencing with a student, take the revision step by step. Is the poem clear? Does it convey the ideas the student wants? Guide the writer to add more information to improve clarity or to take out information that does not enhance the main idea.

Then look at language. Are there any words that seem "tired" or "ordinary"? Can the student remove them or replace them with more vigorous vocabulary?

Many poems benefit from work with line breaks. The best approach is to begin by reading the draft poem aloud. Have the student put a slash mark whenever she hears a pause in her voice – or do it for her. Think about whether she should add punctuation or change the line breaks.

Finally, reach into the poetry toolbox. Has the student used alliteration, onomatopoeia, repetition, similes or rhymes? If not, you may want to suggest one or more to make the poem more interesting and effective.

The following chart is a guideline for assessing student poetry and can provide ideas for improvement.

What Effective Poetry Looks Like

Ideas	Organization	Voice	Word Choice	Sentence Fluency	Conventions
The author seems to have a passion for the topic; or there is an element of surprise or a unique way of expressing a familiar idea.	Ideas are sequenced in a way that balances sound and sense; words and ideas work together; the rhyme scheme or structure is effective.	The poem conveys emotion or feeling; reader connects with the poet.	Words create visual and other sensory images; no unnecessary words or trite expressions are evident.	Line breaks occur at rhythmical and logical places; poem flows smoothly, with a strong rhythm and cadence.	Capitalization and punctuation seem effective and logical; words are spelled appropriately for the writer's developmental level.

Editing and publishing

One advantage of poetry is that the poet has a fair degree of latitude about sentences, capitals and punctuation – otherwise e.e. cummings would not have the reputation he does and Thomas Hardy couldn't have made up new words such as "smalling" where they suited him. On the other hand, cummings and Hardy were both very careful about typesetting and typography, specifying exactly what they wanted to get the effect needed for a particular poem. Encourage your students to take the same care.

Students should read their poems aloud to determine when natural pauses occur. Then they can add commas, semi-colons and periods as necessary. Generally speaking, each line begins with a capital letter, though this is not absolutely necessary with modern verse.

Once students have finished editing their poetry for conventions, it is time to publish. There are many possibilities for sharing published poetry. A "coffee house" with candles and checkered tablecloths is a wonderful atmosphere for a poetry reading. Oral presentations of poetry can be accompanied by music, dance or rhythm effects.

Creating individual poetry anthologies is a popular way to celebrate poetry. Your criteria for the student anthologies will vary, but generally you should consider these questions:

- What is the minimum number of selections?
- How many poems must be written by the student and how many must be selected from other published sources?
- What form of response do you want for the published poems?
- What are your expectations for neatness, word processing, and illustrations?
- Should an introduction, conclusion or reflection be included?

Ideally, you and your students could explore a variety of published anthologies and together create a set of criteria. Here is one possible format:

POETRY ANTHOLOGY

1. The anthology must contain a minimum of <u>five poems that you have written </u> and <u>five poems that other people have written.</u> Poems by others must include the author's name.

2. Every poem by another author must include a response or comment by you, as the anthologist, explaining why it was chosen.

3. Every poem must be word-processed, neatly formatted and printed on a separate page, with appropriate graphics or illustrations. Pages should be numbered.

4. You will follow the usual writing process. Submit the TAG sheet along with your rough draft for 20 percent of your mark. On the final anthology, all of your punctuation, spelling and grammar should be appropriate to style.

5. The anthology must contain these features:
   a. A cover page which includes the title of the anthology and the student's name
   b. A table of contents with page numbers
   c. An introduction presenting an overview of the selections
   d. An alphabetical index of first lines

   Rough draft due: _____
   Editing complete by: _____
   Finished anthology due: _____

Admittedly, it is unlikely that your students will go on to write a great deal of poetry in their adult lives. Nonetheless, the writing skills they learn in attempting poetry – attention to sound, symbolism, meaning and concise expression – will pay big dividends when invested in other genres. In teaching poetry, as in so much else, we are not looking for immediate rewards, but for sustained and deeper growth. Poetry is worth your time teaching; and theirs, learning.

It's Saturday
by Paul, Grade 3

I get up and stretch, I open my eyes
I go to my brother's room and say, "Come on, guys."
But they're snoring, they're deep asleep
they won't even make a peep!

It's 8:00, just 40 minutes left!
The school bus is coming. I better get dressed.
Mom's not up. I better make lunch.
O man! I almost forgot my Cinnamon Toast Crunch.

My siblings get up and watch TV with their blankets and pillows,
I say, "Get up, you lazy fellows!"
They say, "Don't you know?"
"Know what?"
"It's SATURDAY."

I'm Waiting
by Dana, Grade 4

for people to stop killing animals,
for clean water,
for no drugs,
for people to stop swearing,
for starving people to have food,
and then I'll know,
the earth is saved!!

Two Friends
by Danielle, Grade 5

Danielle and Jade have:
two best-friend necklaces
four pigtails
two blue shirts
and two pairs of black pants
two watches
ten red nails and ten purple ones
at least ten pairs of shoes
two brown heads
one head of long hair and
one head of short
two trampolines
and one AWESOME friendship!

Maui Dreams
by Jennifer, Grade 6

I watch the morning sun
set the sky on fire
over the mountain.

I bask on the beach,
soaking up the sun.
I splash in the salty surf.

I scan the horizon
for the silhouettes of breaching whales
and diving dolphins.

Black sand tickles my toes
as I stroll along the beach.
Windsurfers' neon sails
skim across the shimmering sea.

I watch the sun
drop below the horizon
leaving the island in darkness.

The alarm clock rings.
It's back to reality.
Fifty below in Saskatchewan.

Asleep
by Laura, Grade 7

A blanket of darkness covers the land.
There must be a hole
in the afghan of night.
For I see light.
The moon is our pillow.
The land is asleep.
The rooster crows and the sun is turned on.
We get up to start a bright new day.

Student Writing

10

Putting It All Together – The Multi-genre Project

"A multigenre paper is composed of many genres and subgenres, each piece self-contained, making a point of its own, yet connected by theme or topic and sometimes by language, images and content." – Tom Romano

A multi-genre project is a collection of writing pieces in different genres and text forms, but all focusing on a single theme. Each genre piece reflects a different facet of the theme, combined into a visual presentation that may end up as a display, a scrapbook or a Web site. We look at the multi-genre project as a culmination of a year's work in writing. It enables students to demonstrate their knowledge of different text forms as they explore a topic that they care about. Moreover, it requires them to plan and implement an independent project that displays what they have learned throughout the year. What better way to finish June than with an impressive display of student work all around the classroom and on your school Web site!

Teaching the Multi-genre Project

Before assigning this project to your students, you will want to think carefully about your goals and expectations for them and your own role in teaching and evaluating the project. Consider the following questions:

- What learning objectives will this project address?
- What are my expectations for the number of writing pieces and the overall presentation of the multi-genre project?
- What teaching and resources do I need to provide in order to help the students succeed in their projects?
- How much class time am I going to allocate to work on this project?
- How am I going to evaluate the project and the students' progress toward the learning objectives?

Determine learning objectives

What do you want the students to learn from this project? Your decisions about learning objectives will guide the implementation of the project as well as your evaluation process. Key learning objectives for a project such as this might include the following:

Although a project such as this could address dozens of curricular goals, you will probably want to focus on no more than five or six that you will evaluate at the end of the project.

- Students will create an integrated textual and visual presentation that reflects different aspects of a chosen theme.
- Students will demonstrate their abilities to write a variety of text forms to suit different purposes.
- Students will communicate the intended message with clarity and style.
- Students will organize their time effectively and demonstrate use of the writing process.

Address assessment and evaluation first

How will you know whether the students have achieved the intended objectives? Assessment tools and techniques should be chosen to match the objectives. You might use checklists and anecdotal notes to assess process. Rubrics are effective tools for evaluating both process and product. An analytic rubric may be designed to match the objectives you have laid out. Ideally, you can develop the rubric with the students, so they have an investment in the process and understand the process by which they will be evaluated. If you use a prepared rubric, such as the one provided at the end of this chapter, the criteria for evaluation should be shared with your students at the outset.

Set project requirements

What parts of the assignment will be compulsory for all students? What parts will be optional or open to choice? Are there any writing pieces that you will want to assess separately, along with evidence of process? As with all assignments, you will avoid problems if you make your expectations clear from the start.

We recommend assigning at least two "process" pieces in genres you have studied in class. In other words, you will evaluate all steps of the process, even though only the final copy will appear as part of the presentation. This structure also helps students pace themselves in completing all components of the project.

In general, a project should include a piece from four of the six genres we have presented in this book and at least four "minor" pieces such as invitations, postcards, recipes, or glossaries. Encourage students to keep all their written pieces to no more than one or two pages in length. Remind them that visuals and graphics are an important part of the overall presentation.

Lori also likes to have her students include a reflective piece on what they have learned from this project. A student might comment on why she chose her theme, what she learned about it and what she learned about herself as a writer.

Consider what students need to know

You have already taught the major writing genres. Are there any other skills or concepts your students will need to know in order to create the project? Mini-lessons on inserting computer graphics into a text or balancing visuals and text on a page may be in order for some or all of your students. Don't feel that you have to do it all; a guest speaker such as a graphic designer or even some of your own students may be able to help with this instruction.

A timeline with deadlines along the way is also an essential tool – to prevent students from spending two weeks on their cover page, then scrambling to complete the writing!

Many students in elementary and middle school do not have the skills to organize and manage a long-term project such as the multi-genre on their own. You'll have to guide them in planning their projects, finding resources, and organizing their ideas. Make sure to design the project and timeline so that students have the opportunity to go through the processes of planning, drafting, revising, editing and publishing. A planner with ongoing deadlines, such as the one found on page 162, will help students balance their time and prevent the common problem of spending two weeks on a cover page, then scrambling to complete the rest of the project.

Samples of good multi-genre projects are essential teaching tools. We recommend that you create a project of your own – as a model and as a way to anticipate student struggles with the project – then get permission from your students to keep samples of excellent projects to use in subsequent years. An Internet search of "Multi-genre Projects" will yield many examples of varying degrees of quality.

As the students work, be sure to monitor their progress and provide ongoing conferences and feedback. Doing this will help you plan instruction as needed for individuals and groups.

Celebrate the projects

When the projects are completed, invite other classes or parents to join you for a celebration of the work. Set up a display where each student can stand by his or her project to explain and answer questions as visitors circulate. It is a wonderful way to finish up the school year – and most of your students will have a treasure they will save for a long time to come.

From Conception to Celebration

It is not enough to just assign a project of this magnitude. You will need to provide explicit instruction and support along the way. The following steps may be used to guide students through the process.

Introduce the task

Michael Ondaatje's *Billy the Kid* is an excellent example of multi-genre writing for adults.

Show examples of what a multi-genre project looks like and establish the parameters of the assignment. Walk students through the assignment guidelines and the due dates. Tell your students which components will be done in class and what they will have to do on their own. Make sure they understand the evaluation process and criteria.

Together with the students, create lists of possible genres and formats, as well as resources available in your school and nearby. If your students don't know how to access Internet information, library card catalogues, indices and tables of contents, it is important to take time to teach them these skills.

Guide students in developing their project proposals

A project proposal helps writers organize their thinking, plan their time and resources, and focus their energies. Of course, the proposal is just a

Single pieces in a multi-genre project should not be long – one or two pages are adequate. Remember that the project is a presentation piece. The audience will not likely expect – or have the time – to read several pages.

guideline that can and likely will be changed as the work is done, but students should know what their goal is before they can set off.

There are two components to the proposal: choosing a topic and planning the writing pieces that will be part of the project.

Whether you are limiting topics to certain themes or leaving the choice wide open, it is important to give students some guidance. Some topics lend themselves more readily to multi-genre writing than others. All writing is best if the writer chooses topics he cares and knows something about, even if research is still required for the project. While individual writing pieces work best with "skinny" topics, students will want something more general for the multi-genre project. Here are some themes that work well for student projects:

- Historical events: the September 11 terrorist attacks, the Holocaust, the Great Depression, the walk on the moon
- Places: Paris, the Pyramids, the ocean, the Arctic
- Biographies of famous people: Mozart, Galileo, Mother Teresa, Shakespeare
- Family and friends: family history, family reunions, traditions, siblings
- Issues and topics of interest: witchcraft, cloning, cancer, divorce, space travel, animals, sports, fashion
- Universal themes: love, humor, the environment, peace, friendship

You and your students have already studied some major writing forms, such as personal memoir, fictional narrative, informational report, procedure, poem and opinion piece. You may want to review some of the various forms of each: a diary, a newspaper article, a brochure, a biographical sketch, an editorial, a letter to the editor. "Possible Text Forms for Multi-genre Projects," on page 163, will give you a starting point to brainstorm other forms of writing that students might choose to use. It will help some students to outline the information they want to include in the project and choose text forms that will convey that information most effectively. The examples on pages 159 to 161 will also be helpful.

Don't be surprised if your students include more than the minimum number of writing pieces. When they discover the ease of writing such pieces as invitations, glossaries or postcards, you'll find that the pieces start spilling into their folders, shoeboxes or Web sites.

It's always a good idea for students to have some sense of how the final project will look: displays, Web sites, and scrapbooks are popular choices. Some students like to store their projects in a decorated box or folder.

Increasingly, the Web site is a popular form for display because it can accommodate both text and visuals with ease. The problem, of course, is uploading and editing a Web site, tasks that often require considerable parent support. Web sites give students a chance to interlink their work with other sites, as well as to incorporate PowerPoint and Flash displays if the kids are Web savvy. Unfortunately, a single Web page can only handle about 125 words of text in a reasonable font size, so they are not very suitable for long stories or extended prose. Any form of presentation, as your students will learn, has its strengths and weaknesses. You should always allow your students to change their minds on presentation as their projects develop, but starting with some end in mind helps provide a focus.

Here is a sample project proposal form:

```
┌─────────────────────────────────────────────────────────────────┐
│                                                                 │
│  Project proposal by  _____  │
│                                                                 │
│  Topic:  _____ │
│                                                                 │
│                                                                 │
│  Text Forms/Genres:                      Topics:                │
│                                                                 │
│  Narrative  _____             _____  │
│                                                                 │
│  Expository  _____             _____  │
│                                                                 │
│  _____               _____  │
│                                                                 │
│  _____               _____  │
│                                                                 │
│  _____               _____  │
│                                                                 │
│  _____               _____  │
│                                                                 │
│  Form the final presentation may take:  _____  │
│                                                                 │
└─────────────────────────────────────────────────────────────────┘
```

Provide time and support for student writing

Because students will be working on their own for most of this task, it's a good idea to establish a series of deadlines to help them stay on track. It is also valuable to provide access to word processors for this project.

While students are writing, circulate among them to provide ongoing suggestions and support. It is essential that the students receive feedback on their work *during* the process, so that they can make improvements as they work. Comments after the project is turned in contribute nothing to the quality of the assignment and little to the student's overall growth in writing. Teacher conferencing also helps students who struggle with organizational skills to keep on track. Plan to conference with every student at least twice during the term of the project.

Maintain checklists and anecdotal records of students' progress as they work. Doing so will make planning for instruction and assessment much more efficient.

Invite celebration and response

Plan a special event to celebrate the multi-genre projects. Invite parents and other classes to view and respond to the projects.

Allow the students to practise reporting on their projects for others in the class. Each project might be accompanied by a Reader's Comments sheet. Teach students to write only positive comments and model appropriate types of responses.

Evaluating the Multi-genre Project

"The Multi-genre Project Assignment" sheet on page 162 is one assessment guide. You may also want to include peer- and self-evaluations, requiring support or justification for the analyses. The Six Traits rubrics described in Chapter 3 are excellent tools for student- and teacher-evaluation of individual writing pieces. The following rubric may be used to score the project holistically.

Rubric for Holistic Scoring

Exemplary (32–40 marks)	Well Done (24–32 marks)	Below Standard (Fewer than 24 marks)
• Project exceeds required number of pieces. • The treatment of theme is original. • Writing is well crafted. • Conventions are correct. • Visual representations (graphics, etc.) communicate intended message in a unique way.	• All writing is linked to theme. • Writing demonstrates appropriate content and craft. • Expected number of genre pieces are provided. • Visual presentation is attractive. • Conventions are correct.	• Tasks are incomplete. • Connection to topic may be mundane or not evident. • There is an inadequate use of conventions. • Visual component is missing or inadequate.

Given the extended size of a multi-genre project, student samples can be presented only in outline form. Still, we hope that the following three outlines give you an idea of the variety of genres, forms and presentations possible.

In our experience, each student writer has strengths in different genres and forms. The girl who crafts wonderful poems may not be as strong in writing an opinion piece; the boy who creates wonderful short procedural pieces may seize up when asked to write a short story. The multi-genre project provides students with an opportunity to bring forward the genres at which they excel and to do so in a very public way. Give your students a chance to let their best works shine and they will never forget the skills you taught them or the applause you brought their way.

Bees

Web-based multi-genre project
by Corey, Grade 4
(with lots of help from his parents)

- Information piece: Honeybees
- Quiz: What Do You Know About Bees?
- Poem: Busy as a Bee
- Interview: Mr. Sorenson, a Real Beekeeper

- Opinion: Should Bees Go into Space?
- Diagram: A Beehive
- Memoir: The Day I Was Stung
- Short story: The Bees Are Coming!
- Song: Beehive Rap

By Corey

- Honeybees
- Quiz: What Do You Know About Bees?
- Poem: Busy as a Bee
- Interview: Mr. Sorenson, a Real Beekeeper
- Opinion: Should Bees Go Into Space?
- Diagram: A beehive
- Memoir: The Day I Was Stung
- Short Story: The Bees are Coming!
- Beehive Rap
- Song: Beehive

Bees have been making honey for 150 million years. They don't make it just for us. Bees make honey for their own use in the winter, and for other animals. They make much more honey than they can eat.

There are different kinds of bees in a beehive. There are drones, workers and a Queen. Each of . . .

Interview with a Beekeeper

Mr. Sorenson is a real beekeeper. He has over 20 bee hives on his farm. Each hive has about 5000 bees. The beehives make over 200 jars of honey each year that Mr. Sorenson sells in town.

Q: Are you afraid of bees?

No Bees in Space!

In 2003, NASA sent hundreds of spice bees into space on the last Challenger mission. The bees were part of an experiment, but they all died when the space shuttle exploded.

Is it fair to risk bees by sending them to outer space? I say no. Bees are living beings, just like . . .

Galileo
Outline for a multi-genre work
by Keith, Grade 6

Information	Writing piece
Galileo was born in Pisa, Italy, in 1520 and lived in Florence, Sienna, Padua, Venice and Rome.	Birth certificate Map of Italy with cities marked
In 1609 Galileo invented the telescope.	Labeled diagram of a telescope
Galileo made many discoveries with his telescope, including four moons of Jupiter, the Milky Way was made up of tiny stars, mountains on the moon.	Informational report Journal or scientific log Timeline
Galileo fell into disfavor with the Catholic Church and was imprisoned for life because he wrote that the earth revolved around the sun.	Persuasive text to convince the Pope to release him
Galileo's greatest supporter was his daughter Virginia, a nun.	Short story telling about Galileo from Virginia's perspective Eulogy
In 1992, Pope John Paul II exonerated Galileo.	Declaration from the Pope on a scroll

A Trip to the Emerald Isle
by Jennifer, Grade 9

(Jennifer took the trip with her mother the previous summer.)
Print pieces included the following:

- Short story: "Thoughts on Ireland"
- Personal memoir: "The Queen of Canada"
- Dictionary: "Irish Words and Phrases"
- Picture with captions: "Leprechaun"
- Postcard from Ireland
- Brochure: "A Dublin Literary Tour"
- Poem: "My Grandfather was an Irishman"
- Photo-Journal
- Invitation: "Invitation to a Party at Dublin Castle"
- Illuminated manuscript (based on the Book of Kells)

The Multi-genre Project Assignment

(3–4 weeks)

Project Component	What to Consider	Due Date	Mark Value
1. Proposal	• Choose your topic. • Indicate writing forms you plan to use.		0
2. Process piece #1: Narrative	• Planning. • Rough draft with revisions for feedback (Six Traits rubric) • Final copy in finished project (1–2 pages)		20
3. Process piece #2: Expository or Informational	• Planning • Rough draft with revisions for feedback (Six Traits rubric) • Final copy in finished project (1–2 pages)		20
4. *At least four* additional writing pieces, of different forms, including a visual component	• Hand in with final project. • Evaluation is based on relevance to topic, originality, quality, and presentation (see rubric). • Pieces will not be evaluated separately; there will be one mark for the group. • More than four pieces will be accepted.		40
5. Reflective piece	• What did you know before you started? • What did you learn? • Why did you choose these formats? • How do they fit together? • What did you learn about yourself as a writer?		10
6. Final product	• neatness, presentation • conventions		10
TOTAL			100

Possible Text Forms for Multi-genre Projects

Advertisement
Advice column
Anecdote
Announcement
Apology
Article
Autobiographical sketch
Ballad
Biographical sketch
Birth announcement
Campaign speech
Cartoon
Character sketch
Chart
Description
Dialogue
Diary entry
Directions
Essay
Eulogy
Fable or fairy tale
Fact sheet
Family tree
Greeting card
Game rules
Glossary or dictionary
Horoscope
How-to
Interview
Invitation
Joke
Legend or myth
Letter of complaint
Letter to the editor
List

Magazine article
Map with labels
Memoir
News article
Obituary
Opinion piece
Parody
Personal ad
Petition
Picture book
Picture with caption or label
Poem
Position statement
Postcard
Poster
PowerPoint presentation
Quiz
Rap
Recipe
Report/Research paper
Review — Book, Movie, CD
Riddles
Script
Short story
Song
Speech
Sports column
Statement of belief
Summary
Tall tale
Thesaurus
Want ad
Wanted poster
Wish list

Annotated Bibliography

There are many good professional books on teaching writing. Here are some of our favorites.

Atwell, Nancy. 1998. *In the Middle: New Understandings about Writing, Reading and Learning.* 2d ed. Portsmouth, NH: Heinemann.
> In this revised edition of the classic text on reading and Writing Workshop with adolescents, Atwell reminds teachers to "teach with a capital T."

Calkins, Lucy McCormick. 1994. *The Art of Teaching Writing.* Portsmouth, NH: Heinemann.
> This wonderful book was the first to introduce the "mini-lesson."

Cecil, Nancy Lee. 1994. *For the Love of Language.* Winnipeg, MB: Portage & Main Press.
> Various scaffolds and frameworks to help students write free verse poetry

Culham, Ruth. 2002. *The 6+1 Traits of Writing.* New York: Scholastic Inc.
> Numerous ideas for teaching and assessing each of the traits from an author who was a "pioneering researcher" of the 6+1 Traits model

Education Department of Western Australia. 1994. *First Steps Writing Resource Book.*
> A writing resource that links assessment and teaching through various text forms

Fletcher, Ralph, and JoAnn Portalupi. 2000. *Craft Lessons.* Portland, ME: Stenhouse Publishers.
> A collection of mini-lessons for teaching various elements of writer's craft to writers of all ages

Gillet, Jean Wallace, and Beverly Lynn. 2001. *Directing the Writing Workshop.* New York: The Guilford Press.
> A comprehensive general text for teaching writing

Graves, Donald. 1994. *A Fresh Look at Writing.* Portsmouth, NH: Heinemann.
> Sometimes called "the father of the writing process," Graves offers detailed instructions for setting up a Writing Workshop in the classroom.

Laase, Lois, and Joan Clemmons. 1998. *Helping Students Write the Best Research Reports Ever.* New York: Scholastic Professional Books.
> Mini-lessons and activities for helping students conduct research and write informational reports

Lane, Barry. 1999. *After "The End": Teaching and Learning Creative Revision*. Shoreham, VT: Discover Writing Press.

A unique resource for teaching the tools of revision

Lane, Barry, and Gretchen Bernabei. 2001. *Why We Must Run with Scissors*. Shoreham, VT: Discover Writing Press.

Lessons and student writing samples for teaching persuasive writing

Mariconda, Barbara. 1999. *The Most Wonderful Writing Lessons Ever*. New York: Scholastic Professional Books.

Practical ideas for crafting narrative writing

_____. 2001. *Step-by-Step Strategies for Teaching Expository Writing*. New York: Scholastic Professional Books.

From planning to publication, a detailed outline for teaching informational writing

Nickelsen, LeAnn. 2001. *Teaching Elaboration and Word Choice*. New York: Scholastic Professional Books.

Ideas for teaching students to use powerful and effective vocabulary in their writing.

Olness, Rebecca (in press). *Using Literature to Enhance Writing Instruction*. Newark, DE: International Reading Association.

Literature links for teaching ideas, organization, voice, word choice, sentence fluency and conventions in writing

Robb, Laura. 1999. *Brighten Up Boring Beginnings and Other Quick Writing Lessons*. New York: Scholastic Professional Books.

Eighteen mini-lessons for teaching the writer's craft

_____. 2001. *Grammar Lessons and Strategies*. New York: Scholastic Professional Books.

From parts of speech to punctuation, 20 mini-lessons for teaching conventions

Schaefer, Lola. 2001. *Teaching Narrative Writing: The Tools That Work for Every Student*. New York: Scholastic Professional Books.

Ideas for planning, drafting, revising, editing and publishing fictional narratives

Spandel, Vicki. 2001. *Creating Writers (Through 6-Trait Writing Assessment and Instruction)*. 3rd ed. New York: Addison-Wesley Longman.

The original and most comprehensive resource on Six Traits rubrics and how to use them

Index